Instructional Leadership for School Improvement

Sally J. Zepeda

EYE ON EDUCATION

6 DEPOT WAY WEST, SUITE 106

LARCHMONT, NY 10538

(914) 833–0551

(914) 833–0761 fax

www.eyeoneducation.com

Library of Congress Cataloging-in-Publication Data

Zepeda, Sally J., 1956–
    Instructional leadership for school improvement / Sally J. Zepeda.
    p.cm.
    Includes bibliographical references and index.
    ISBN 1-903556-72-1
    1. Educational leadership—United States. 2. School improvement programs—United States. 3. School principals—United States. 4. Teachers—Training of—United States. I. Title.

    LB2822.82.Z46   2003
    371.2'03—dc22

                                                                2003064215

10 9 8 7 6 5 4 3 2 1

Editorial and production services provided by
Richard H. Adin Freelance Editorial Services
52 Oakwood Blvd., Poughkeepsie, NY 12603-4112
(845-471-3566)

Also Available from EYE ON EDUCATION

The Principal as Instructional Leader:
A Handbook for Supervisors
Sally J. Zepeda

Instructional Supervision: Applying Concepts and Tools
Sally J. Zepeda

The Call to Teacher Leadership
Sally J. Zepeda, R. Stewart Mayers, & Brad N. Benson

101 "Answers" for New Teachers and Their Mentors:
Effective Teaching Tips for Daily Classroom Use
Annette L. Breaux

What Great Principals Do Differently:
15 Things That Matter Most
Todd Whitaker

What Great Teachers Do Differently:
14 Things That Matter Most
Todd Whitaker

Staff Development: Practices That Promote
Leadership in Learning Communities
Sally J. Zepeda

Handbook on Teacher Evaluation:
Assessing and Improving Performance
James H. Stronge and Pamela D. Tucker

Handbook on Educational Specialist Evaluation:
Assessing and Improving Performance
James H. Stronge and Pamela D. Tucker

Dealing with Difficult Teachers, Second Edition
Todd Whitaker

Motivating and Inspiring Teachers:
The Educator's Guide for Building Staff Morale
Whitaker, Whitaker, and Lumpa

Achievement Now! How To Assure No Child is Left Behind
Dr. Donald J. Fielder

Coaching and Mentoring First-year and Student Teachers
India J. Podsen and Vicki Denmark

Teaching Matters:
Motivating & Inspiring Yourself
Todd and Beth Whitaker

Teacher Retention: What Is Your Weakest Link?
India J. Podsen

Differentiated Instruction:
A Guide for Elementary School Teachers
Amy Benjamin

Differentiated Instruction:
A Guide for Middle and High School Teachers
Amy Benjamin

REAL Teachers, REAL Challenges, REAL Solutions:
25 Ways to Handle the Challenges of the Classroom Effectively
Annette L. Breaux and Elizabeth Breaux

From Rigorous Standards to Student
Achievement: A Practical Process
Rettig, McCullough, Santos, and Watson

Data Analysis for Comprehensive
Schoolwide Improvement
Victoria L. Bernhardt

The School Portfolio Toolkit:
A Planning, Implementation, and Evaluation
Guide for Continuous School Improvement
Victoria L. Bernhardt

Dropout Prevention Tools
Franklin P. Schargel

Strategies to Help Solve Our School Dropout Problem
Franklin P. Schargel and Jay Smink

Navigating Comprehensive School Change:
A Guide for the Perplexed
Thomas G. Chenoweth and Robert B. Everhart

Dedication

This book is dedicated to the memory of Millie Brudd, friend, colleague, and a 30-year veteran classroom teacher who in her career spearheaded many school improvement initiatives. Millie, you are sorely missed by your family (Bob, Michael, and Laura) and friends, but know you have left a legacy in the hearts and minds of countless teachers, principals, and students.

About the Author

Sally J. Zepeda has served as a high school teacher, director of special programs, assistant principal, and principal before entering higher education. An associate professor and graduate coordinator in the Department of Educational Administration and Policy, she teaches instructional supervision and other courses related to professional development and school improvement. Dr. Zepeda has written widely about educational administration, supervision of teaching, and the leadership of the principal. Her nine books include *The Principal as Instructional Leader: A Handbook for Supervisors; Instructional Supervision: Applying Tools and Concepts; The Call to Teacher Leadership* (with R. Stewart Mayers and Brad Benson); *Staff Development: Practices That Promote Leadership in Learning Communities; Hands-on Leadership Tools for Principals* (with Raymond Calabrese and Gary Short); *The Reflective Supervisor: A Practical Guide for Educators* (with Raymond Calabrese); *Special Programs in Regular Schools: Historical Foundations, Standards, and Contemporary Issues* (with Michael Langenbach); and *Supervision and Staff Development in the Block* (with R. Stewart Mayers).

Acknowledgments

The professionals who reviewed this manuscript while it was in process selflessly shared their perspectives, and this book is all the stronger because of the insights of the reviewers: David Bower, Elizabeth City, and Gregg Mowen.

The two cases in this book were developed by Dr. Ruth O'Dell, principal of Lindsey Elementary School in Warner Robins, Georgia (Houston County) and Mrs. Karen Yarbrough, principal of Sonny Carter Elementary School, and Ms. Kelly Catherine Nagle, former assistant principal at Sonny Carter Elementary School (Bibb County). The work at Lindsey Elementary School and Sonny Carter Elementary School is a testament that school improvement is a reality and the work of these professionals is representative of the work of principals across the states. Dr. Mike Mattingly, Executive Director of Elementary Operations, Houston County Schools, provided numerous resources and materials from his collection on school improvement.

Garrick Askew, a doctoral student and a research assistant in the Program of Educational Leadership at the University of Georgia provided invaluable assistance as did Dana Bickmore, a former middle and high school principal who is working toward a doctorate in the Department of Elementary Education at the University of Georgia.

Nashette Garrick, a Master's Degree student and my research assistant in the Department of Educational Administration and Policy spent countless hours assisting me in coming to closure on this book.

The many lively discussions about the importance of the work of principals in bringing about school improvement with Bob Sickles made writing this book a pleasurable experience. Many thanks go to Richard Adin for his eye to detail on the final layout and design of this book.

TABLE OF CONTENTS

1

Thinking About School Improvement

In this Chapter...

♦ Accountability
♦ School improvement broadly defined
♦ The work of the principal in school improvement
♦ Overview of the process of school improvement

Introducing School Improvement

What is the work of the principal in championing school improvement? This book attempts to address the myriad responses that could be given to answer this question by exploring school improvement and the work of the principal. The following list highlights the contents of each chapter.

♦ Chapter 1 creates the context for school improvement and outlines the role of the principal, as defined in the chapters that follow.

♦ Chapter 2 explains the principal's role in assessing and building a positive school culture and setting the climate for school improvement.

♦ Chapter 3 explores ways in which the principal can be supportive of and create conditions so that teacher leaders can emerge in the educational setting.

♦ Chapter 4 outlines ways in which the principal can support team building and the work that teams need to tackle during school improvement.

♦ Chapter 5 leads the principal in the planning for school improvement.

♦ Chapter 6 identifies the principal's role in implementing and monitoring school improvement.

School improvement is not a new construct, and principals, who are instructional leaders, have been and will continue to motivate teachers, students, and others toward improvement. Effective principals will not be caught off guard by increased accountability, because these leaders approach school improvement as a constant and prevailing process. School improvement is at the forefront of the work of these principals, and these principals accept that they and their schools can work toward meeting high expectations. As the leaders, principals in schools that are improving must do the following:

- Focus their own and the efforts of others by asking tough questions.

- Track data to provide a basis of reality for the answers to these questions.

- Identify the needs of students through systematic and inclusive means.

- Develop strategies based on research to meet these needs.

- Prioritize the needs of students, teachers, and others who are served by the school.

- Provide teachers with the support and assistance needed to meet the needs of their students.

School improvement is a multifaceted process that never really ends. The process of school improvement is a collaborative effort dependent on a culture and climate that support growth and learning for teachers and the organization. It is not likely that there will be growth and development unless there is alignment of the needs of both the people and the organization itself. Programs and initiatives that forward school improvement for schools labeled as "failing" are based on criteria such as standardized test results; although these programs and initiatives might be noteworthy, they are outside the scope of this book and are, moreover, often implemented as quick fixes.

More than just a commitment to improvement is needed to accomplish school improvement that is lasting and reaches the level of the classroom teacher. Although it falls to the principal to organize, plan, and accept final responsibility for school improvement, it takes teachers to mobilize a plan of improvement. Harris (2002) stresses, "the school improvement research base highlights the centrality of teaching and learning in the pursuit of sustained school improvement" (p. 1). Harris suggests further that the centrality of teaching and learning is related to change, and that for successful school improvement to occur, both the people and the organization must be able to change in ways that align with improvement.

Accountability

Accountability is a reality that school personnel face, and it is doubtful that the press of the accountability movement will waver in the minds and actions of internal and external stakeholders. Although accountability for schools has evolved since the 1960s, the accountability movement has created many zigzags and unlit roads ahead for schools.

A Brief History Leading to the Present Call for High-Stakes Accountability

Essentially, the beginnings of accountability through standards for schools began in 1965 when the U.S. Congress passed the *Elementary and Secondary Education Act* (ESEA) and established Title I of the ESEA, which provided money to support poorly performing students in disadvantaged schools (Popham, 2001; Rudalevige, 2003) Popham (2001) explains how evaluation standards emerged from the passage of ESEA:

> The law required educators receiving ESEA dollars to demonstrate that these funds were being well spent—namely, by evaluating and reporting on the effectiveness of their federally supported programs. According to the new law, if local officials did not formally evaluate the current year's federally subsidized program, then they would not receive next year's ESEA funds. (pp. 8–9)

Popham further relates that

> it should come as no shock that educators who were getting ESEA awards scurried madly about in an effort to document the success of their ESEA-funded programs. And because almost all these programs were aimed directly at improving students' basic skills, the first step for most local educators was to identify suitable tests that could determine whether students were in fact learning the three Rs. (p. 9)

To an extent, the standards of the accountability movement began with the passage of ESEA and the *Title I: Improving The Academic Achievement of the Disadvantaged* provisions that include:

Sec. 1001. Statement of Purpose.

The purpose of this title is to ensure that all children have a fair, equal, and significant opportunity to obtain a high-quality education and reach, at a minimum, proficiency on challenging State academic achievement standards and state academic assessments. This purpose can be accomplished by—

(1) ensuring that high-quality academic assessments, accountability systems, teacher preparation and training, curriculum, and instructional materials are aligned with challenging State academic standards so that students, teachers, parents, and administrators can measure progress against common expectations for student academic achievement;

(2) meeting the educational needs of low-achieving children in our Nation's highest-poverty schools, limited English proficient children, migratory children, children with disabilities, Indian children, neglected or delinquent children, and young children in need of reading assistance;

(3) closing the achievement gap between high- and low-performing children, especially the achievement gaps between minority and nonminority students, and between disadvantaged children and their more advantaged peers;

(4) holding schools, local educational agencies, and States accountable for improving the academic achievement of all students, and identifying and turning around low-performing schools that have failed to provide a high-quality education to their students, while providing alternatives to students in such schools to enable the students to receive a high-quality education;

(5) distributing and targeting resources sufficiently to make a difference to local educational agencies and schools where needs are greatest;

(6) improving and strengthening accountability, teaching, and learning by using State assessment systems designed to ensure that students are meeting challenging State academic achievement and content standards and increasing achievement overall, but especially for the disadvantaged;

(7) providing greater decision making authority and flexibility to schools and teachers in exchange for greater responsibility for student performance;

(8) providing children an enriched and accelerated educational program, including the use of schoolwide programs or additional services that increase the amount and quality of instructional time;

(9) promoting schoolwide reform and ensuring the access of children to effective, scientifically based instructional strategies and challenging academic content;

(10) significantly elevating the quality of instruction by providing staff in participating schools with substantial opportunities for professional development;

(11) coordinating services under all parts of this title with each other, with other educational services, and, to the extent feasible, with other agencies providing services to youth, children, and families; and

(12) affording parents substantial and meaningful opportunities to participate in the education of their children. (Sec. 1001)

Source: http://www.ed.gov/policy/elsec/leg/esea02/pg1.html

Providing fodder for the evolution of the accountability movement were key reports in the 1980s and the 1990s (although now some of the findings in these reports have been challenged) that detailed the abysmal condition of education. In late 1983, the Commission of Excellence issued its report, *A Nation at Risk,* in which it warned that

> the educational foundation of our society was being eroded by a rising tide of mediocrity that threatens our very future as a nation and a people. The report alleged that part of the responsibility of the America's declining productivity in the face of accelerating foreign competition could be traced to the school's poor performance. (p. 3)

The report further declared, "our society and its educational institutions seem to have lost sight of the basic purpose of schooling and of the high expectations and disciplined effort to attain them" (p. 3).

In 1990 the Bush administration issued the report *National Goals for Education* to guide the improvement of education in state and local districts (Rudalevige, 2003). On March 31, 1994, Congress passed *Goals 2000: The Educate America Act,* and according to Rudalevige (2003), this

> signaled a nationwide commitment to standards-based reform. The reauthorization [of the Elementary and Secondary Education Act] required states to develop content and performance standards for K–12 schools. Congress also adopted the notion of "adequate yearly progress," which later became the lynchpin of accountability in the *No Child Left Behind* (NCLB) legislation. States were required to make "continuous and substantial" progress toward the goal of academic proficiency for all students. However, there was no deadline for doing so; indeed, consequences were largely absent from the law (p. 64).

According to archived information at http://www.ed.gov/pubs/G2KReforming/g2ch1.html, the authorization of Goals 2000 was based on recognition of fundamental principles that underlie effective school change: (1) all students can learn; (2) lasting improvements depend on school-based leadership; (3) simultaneous top-down and bottom-up reform is necessary; (4) strategies must be locally developed, comprehensive, and coordinated; and (5) the whole community must be involved in developing strategies for system-wide improvement.

Figure 1.1 highlights *Goals 2000: The Educate America Act.*

No Child Left Behind

The *No Child Left Behind* legislation is perhaps one of the strongest series of mandates that places emphasis on accountability for academic achievement results on the principal. Under the new educational standards introduced by the Bush administration, a top priority is for students to pass state and national achievement tests (Wax, 2002). Principals will be judged as either effective or ineffective leaders based on the results of how students perform on tests. In its efforts to promote school improvement, NCLB currently requires school systems to perform a needs analysis to promote

- ◆ effective professional development activities for both teachers and administrators, heavily emphasizing professional mentoring;

- ◆ the competent use of technology initiatives within school classrooms; and

- ◆ the mastery of challenging state academic content standards, by all students, through the use of scientifically validated teaching and learning techniques.

Figure 1.2 (p. 8) lists the requirements for school districts to comply with NCLB.

One of the many provisions of NCLB is that of choice—the parents of students who are in schools that do not meet "adequate yearly progress" now have the option to send their children to another school in or outside of the system where they are enrolled and request extra assistance in the form of supplemental educational services. Parents now have access to information, and further, NCLB ensures that parents have important, timely information about the schools their children attend.

The standard for accountability has put tremendous stress on school system personnel, especially the principal, who now is held *ultimately* accountable for student achievement. Increased accountability has resulted in the principal assuming a greater degree of responsibility for student achievement than in the past (Cooley & Shen, 2003). School improvement, however, does not have to paralyze schools and their personnel. By now, school systems are scurrying at

Figure 1.1. Goals 2000: The Educate America Act

Goal 1:
School Readiness

By the year 2000, all children in America will start school ready to learn.

Goal 2:
School Completion

By the year 2000, the high school graduation rate will increase to at least 90 percent.

Goal 3:
Student Achievement and Citizenship

By the year 2000, all students will leave grades 4, 8, and 12 having demonstrated competency in challenging subject matter including English, mathematics, science, foreign languages, civics and government, economics, arts, history, and geography, and every school in America will ensure that all students learn to use their minds well, so they may be prepared for responsible citizenship, further learning, and productive employment in our nation's modern economy.

Goal 4:
Teacher Education and Professional Development

By the year 2000, the nation's teaching force will have access to programs for the continued improvement of their professional skills and the opportunity to acquire the knowledge and skills needed to instruct and prepare all American students for the next century.

Goal 5:
Mathematics and Science

By the year 2000, U.S. students will be first in the world in mathematics and science achievement.

Goal 6:
Adult Literacy and Lifelong Learning

By the year 2000, every adult American will be literate and will possess the knowledge and skills necessary to compete in a global economy and exercise the rights and responsibilities of citizenship.

Goal 7:
Safe, Disciplined, and Alcohol- and Drug-Free Schools

By the year 2000, every school in the United States will be free of drugs, violence, and the unauthorized presence of firearms and alcohol and will offer a disciplined environment conducive to learning.

Goal 8:
Parental Participation

By the year 2000, every school will promote partnerships that will increase parental involvement and participation in promoting the social, emotional, and academic growth of children.

Source: http://www.ed.gov/pubs/EPTW/eptwgoal.html

Figure 1.2. Results-Based Accountability—NCLB

Under the No Child Left Behind Act, state and local school districts will be required to

- Create their own standards for what a child should know and learn for all grades.

- Test every student's progress by administering standards based testing to students in each of the three grade spans, 3–5, 6–9, and 10–12.

- Sort test results by socioeconomic status, race, ethnicity, and level of limited English proficiency.

- Make test results public at both the state and local level.

- Make continuous improvement towards achieving state standards.

- Bring all students in all schools up to each state's standard of proficient performance.

- Measure progress by requiring a small percentage of the nation's fourth- and eighth-grade students to take the National Assessment of Educational Progress test in math and reading every other year.

- Face real consequences for failing to meet improvement standards.

Sources: U.S. Department of Education (n.d.). *The No Child Left Behind Act of 2001: Executive Summary.* http://www.ed.gov/offices/OESE/esea/exec-summ.html; U.S. Department of Education (n.d.). *Fact Sheet: The No Child Left Behind Act of 2001.* http://www.ed.gov/offices/OESE/esea/factsheet.html; U.S. Department of Education (n.d.). *Introduction: No Child Left Behind.* http://www.nclb.org/next/overview/index.html

rapid speed to respond and, perhaps in some cases, *react* to the measures of student success in which systems will be judged as effective or ineffective—passing or failing. Indeed, the stakes are high.

School Improvement Broadly Defined

Unfortunately, there is not a neat and all-encompassing definition of school improvement, and Seashore-Louis and colleagues (1999) assert that the term "school improvement" is ambiguous and problematic to define (p. 251). The ambiguity in defining school improvement is related to the uniqueness of the school setting and the students served within each building. Dimmock (2002) explains that "attention is currently turning to how schools might redesign themselves to best serve their students in full recognition that each school is a unique mix of students and contextual conditions" that affect school improvement efforts (p. 141).

Given the contextual nature of school and the myriad variables that influence school improvement efforts, leaders scan the environment, looking for markers that define the context of the school, the characteristics of the people whom the school serves, and the characteristics of the teachers and other school personnel who serve students. The information shown in Figure 1.3, examining for now the broad aspects of the school context and the characteristics of the people within the school community, can help the principal to scan the school environment.. The principal will be guided through a more extensive scan and analysis of the school environment in Chapter 2.

Figure 1.3. Scanning the Environment for Contextual Variables—School Context and Characteristics

School Context

School Location
♦ urban, suburban, rural

School Level
♦ high school, elementary, middle school

School Type
♦ public, private, parochial, military, charter, theme

School Demographics
♦ number of students, number of teachers

Unique and Emerging Programs
♦ before and after school programs, summer programs, evening programs for students and parents

Characteristics

Students
♦ percentage of students receiving free and reduced meals, socioeconomic status of students, students reading below grade level, number of semester failures in key areas (math, English, science), number of students receiving special assistance (special education, ESOL) and involved in support programs

Teachers
♦ attrition rates, number of teachers with less than six years in the profession, number of teachers about ready to retire, education levels (beyond the bachelors degree), staff development opportunities provided throughout the school year

The variables listed in Figure 1.3 influence school improvement, but there are numerous other variables to take into account.

School improvement is more than a phrase; school improvement is a journey from the here and now to a future destination. School improvement efforts should be directed by the questions:

- What is it that we want to become?

- What is best for students?

- What in the environment needs to change to bring about school improvement?

Just like travelers, schools need a roadmap and a compass to make the journey toward school improvement more direct. The roadmap is the school improvement plan, and the goals serve as the compass. Because school improvement is linked to change, it is just as important to have a credible leader to shepherd the school through the turbulence of achieving school improvement.

Universal rules and formulas that encompass school improvement do not exist, in that a plan developed for one school may not work for another school. This lack of applicability across school systems exists, in part, because school improvement addresses gaps—needs—that are as individualistic as the schools for which the plans are developed. Development is the key word in school improvement, as Tobergate and Curtis (2002) assert: "School improvement begins with development—development of people and the school culture to keep the organization vibrant and prepared to meet new needs and challenges" (p. 771).

School improvement is a type of purposeful change, and Harris (2002) believes "successful school improvement is dependent upon the school's ability to manage change and development" (p. 2). The purposeful nature of change and school improvement is critical to distinguish as change as envisioned by Harris is related directly to building capacity by "enhancing student achievement and strengthening the school's capacity for change" (p. 50). Earlier, Harris (2000) reported, "Much of the early school improvement work tended to concentrate upon school-level change. However, subsequent work has recognized the importance of encouraging school-level, teacher-level, and classroom-level change" (p. 6).

To this end, school improvement that is not rooted in changes in classroom practices will more than likely not endure. However, McTighe and Thomas (2003) report that there are two types of school improvement—in the classroom and throughout the school—and that both types of improvement need to be melded, "Schools can integrate these two approaches" (p. 52). It is not likely that change alone in the classroom will bring about improvement without changes in the structure of the school and the *ways things are done*. Tobergate and Curtis (2002) summarize the absoluteness of understanding change and the school improvement process: "It involves recognizing the need for change, understanding the change and building support structures that lead to focused change and school improvement" (p. 771).

The focus on change and the emphasis on the need to reach school improvement from the classroom upward "necessitate a reconceptualization of leadership where teachers and managers engage in shared decision-making and risk-taking. The emphasis is upon active and participatory leadership in school improvement work, rather than top-down delegation" as is found in too many schools (Harris, 2000, p. 6).

There has been much analysis of the history of school improvement (Dimmock, 2002; Hopkins & Reynolds, 2001). Hopkins and Reynolds (2001) indicate that currently school improvement is concerned with the following:

- Increased focus on student outcomes

- Teachers' instructional and behavioral practices targeted for inspection

- Knowledge base of the research and best practices supported by an infrastructure that allows for better utilization

- Increased awareness of building capacity, including strategic planning, staff development, and the use of outside agencies

- Quality measured in a manner that uses both qualitative and quantitative research data

- Organizational control factor that ensures consistency in practice among all members of program implementation

- Balance between creating a vision and creating the support mechanisms to carry it out

- Increased practice of ensuring that there is adequate and appropriate training and professional development for all members of the improvement program

Bruce Hammonds and Wayne Morris of leading-learning.co.nz assert there are six major factors that contribute to school improvement, and these factors are, in part, within the purview of the principal to enhance.

Six Factors Contributing to Improving Schools

1. *Improving schools have clear sense of direction.* They place a premium on effective leadership and on a management approach that can generate a vision of the future and commitment to the schools' direction.

2. *Once the vision has been established, improving schools practice fearlessness and recognize they cannot do perfectly all the things that external organizations ask of them.* They make choices. They take risks.

3. *When improving schools know what they intend to do (and what they are not going to do), they get clear targets for themselves.* They identify time scales, success criteria, and resources—and the staff necessary to achieve them. Monitoring the implementation of agreed-on targets is vital, and the focus of these targets should be on improving student achievement in identified areas of concern.

4. *Openness about performance data within schools is vital.* Discussion about approaches to learning is an important feature of successful schools. Effective schools engage in "restless" self-examination.

5. *Successful schools require learning staffs, which in turn require planned professional development strategies related to the schools' development plans and performance appraisals.* Successful staff members learn from a culture that values continually improving everyday events and processes. Classroom observations have been shown to be the greatest benefit of teacher appraisal systems.

6. *It is good practice for schools to regard all their staff, not just the teachers, as members of the learning community.*

Source: http://www.leading-learning.co.nz/school-vision/six-factors.html. Used with permission.

The Work of the Principal in School Improvement

Student achievement is the cornerstone of the success of principals, and teachers are a key factor in the area of student performance (Hallinger & Heck, 1998; Murphy & Louis, 1994; Wax, 2002). If the principal's success depends on teacher and student performance, the principal's approach as an instructional leader is crucial to promote student achievement. Hallinger and Heck (1998) reviewed quantitative research from 1980 to 1995 pertaining to the relationship between principal leadership and student achievement. Their review concluded that principals do affect school achievement.

The principal can influence student-learning outcomes by setting the school's goals and by promoting effective instructional practices. Collaborative goal setting by the principal underscores his or her ability to focus others on the school's improvement plan. According to Fullan (2002), the instructional leader must be more than just a charismatic leader; and Hallinger, Bickman, and Davis (1996) conclude that effective principals are simultaneously able to implement educational programs while building relationships with their staff. The principal, according to Bernauer (2002), "must exhibit persistence rather than opting for the quick fix" (p. 89) in moving a school toward school improvement.

School improvement will more than likely endure with and through teachers and the work that they can accomplish in the classroom—improved teaching, an enhanced curriculum, and aligned assessment of student learning. To make these improvements, one classroom at a time, teachers need support from the principal. Baker (1997, p. 1) asserts that school leaders can increase the likelihood of long-term success and improvement through the following:

- Shared decision making
- Coordinated staff development
- Strategic plans and small-win tactics
- Persistence for the long term

The early research of McInerney and Leach (1992) illustrates certain principal behavior associated with successful implementation of school improvement efforts. These behaviors include facilitative rather than directive behaviors, promotion of teacher leadership in the development and assessment of school improvement plans, and a culture that fosters collaboration. McGuire (2001, pp. 15–16) indicates that leaders have essential knowledge and skills for effective school leadership:

- Leaders know and understand what it means and what it *takes* to be a leader. Leadership is the act of identifying important goals and then motivating and enabling others to devote themselves and all necessary resources to achievement. It includes summoning oneself and others to learn and adapt to the new situation represented by the goal.

- Leaders have a vision for schools that they constantly share and promote. Leaders have a vision of the ideal, can articulate this vision to any audience, and work diligently to make it a reality. Leaders also know how to build on and sustain a vision that preceded them.

- Leaders communicate clearly and effectively. Leaders possess effective writing and presentation skills. They express themselves clearly, are confident, and are capable of responding to the hard questions in a public forum. They are also direct and precise questioners, always seeking understanding.

- Leaders collaborate and cooperate with others. Leaders communicate high expectations and provide accurate information to foster understanding and to maintain trust and confidence. Leaders reach out to others for support and assistance, build partnerships, secure resources, and share credit for success and accomplishments.

♦ Leaders preserve and take the long view. Leaders build institutions that endure. They "stay the course," maintain focus, and anticipate and work to overcome resistance. They create capacity within the organization to achieve and sustain its vision.

♦ Leaders support, develop, and nurture staff. Leaders set a standard for ethical behavior. They seek diverse perspectives and alternative points of view. They encourage initiative, innovation, collaboration, and a strong work ethic. Leaders expect and provide opportunities for staff to engage in continuous personal and professional growth.

♦ Leaders hold themselves and others responsible and accountable. Leaders embrace and adhere to comprehensive planning that improves the organization. They use data to determine the present state of the organization, identify root-cause problems, propose solutions, and validate accomplishments.

♦ Leaders never stop learning and honing their skills. Leaders are introspective and reflective. Leaders ask questions and seek answers. Leaders in education are familiar with current research and best practice, not only in education, but also in other related fields.

♦ Leaders have the courage to take informed risks. Leaders embrace informed, planned change and recognize that everyone may not support change. Leaders work to win support and are willing to take action in support of their vision even in the face of opposition.

The research of Tobergate and Curtis (2002) assert that there are five behaviors that effective principals exhibit to support school improvement:

1. Build relationships.
2. Recognize the need.
3. Understand change.
4. Build support structures.
5. Create the new focus. (p. 772)

Perhaps a sixth item should be the building of learning communities.

The Power of Relationships

Teachers will look to the principal for affirmation of their efforts at improvement. To this end, the principal needs to view school improvement as an opportunity to celebrate success, build relationships, appraise honestly where teachers and the school are, and forge a credible and meaningful plan for improvement. The school improvement process provides an opportunity for the principal to share power through openness, dialogue, and a sincere desire to build trust.

Leaders build authentic relationships with teachers, students, staff, and other stakeholders, and effective leaders work to promote an environment that support:

♦ *Interaction and participation.* People have many opportunities and reasons to come together in deliberation, association, and action.

♦ *Interdependence.* These associations and actions both promote and depend on mutual needs and commitments.

♦ *Shared interests and beliefs.* People share perspectives, values, understandings, and commitment to common purposes.

♦ *Concern for individual and minority views.* Individual differences are embraced through critical reflection and mechanisms for dissent and lead to growth through the new perspectives they foster.

♦ *Meaningful relationships.* Interactions reflect a commitment to caring, sustaining relationships. (Westheimer, 1998, p. 17, emphasis in the original)

Fullan (2002) believes that building relationships is a prerequisite to efforts to improve schools:

The single factor common to successful change is that relationships improve. If relationships improve, schools get better. If relationships remain the same or get worse, ground is lost. Thus, leaders build relationships with diverse people and groups—especially with people who think differently. (p. 18)

Given the complexities with bringing about school improvement, cohesion is needed, and cohesion is built on more than linking the work of instructional leadership and the management of school improvement tasks. A more powerful force, relationships with others, builds cohesion, and this *connective leadership* is what will help to bind people and their values to the work they do in the process of improving schools and working with one another. Komives (1994) credits Lipman-Bluemen (1989) with coining the term *connective leadership*, and she reports that connective leaders: (1) link people with each other, forming communities and teams that work effectively together, and (2) link people with goals, ideas, and visions built from their shared dreams (p. 50).

Connectivity promotes the ability of the instructional leader to focus squarely on learning while simultaneously leading school personnel. Effective instructional leaders are able first to master and then to transcend the technical aspects of management so that they can

♦ Lead schools in a way that places student and adult learning at the center.

♦ Set high expectations and standards for the academic and social development of all students and the performance of adults.

♦ Demand content and instruction that ensure student achievement of agreed-upon academic standards.

♦ Create a culture of continuous adult learning tied to student learning and other school goals.

♦ Use multiple sources of data as diagnostic tools to assess, identify, and apply instructional improvement.

♦ Actively engage the community to create shared responsibility for student and school success (National Association of Elementary School Principals, 2001).

Effective Leaders Promote Learning Communities

School improvement as a change strategy requires that teachers and administrators work with one another in fundamentally different ways. The development of a learning community can help to unify school improvement efforts. Oxley (1997) indicates that learning communities as a restructuring effort need "a unifying conceptual framework that binds them together into a coherent program of schoolwide restructuring" (p. 625). Learning communities that endure are grounded in three foundations: (1) a culture based on human values, (2) a set of practices for generative conversation, and (3) a capacity to see and work with the flow of life as a system (Kofman & Senge, 1993, p. 12). Generative conversation in a learning community acts as the glue to "affirm its values and its membership, and infuse it with the energy, imagination, and commitment of the group" (Sterline, 1998, p. 66).

The Process of School Improvement

The process of school improvement is multifaceted and comprises broad areas such as organizing and planning for school improvement, and implementing and monitoring school improvement efforts. Within each of these broad areas are myriad processes such as collecting and analyzing data, developing goals, and communicating with stakeholders about the work of the school improvement team. Figure 1.4 depicts the cyclical nature of school improvement.

Figure 1.4. The Cyclical Nature of School Improvement

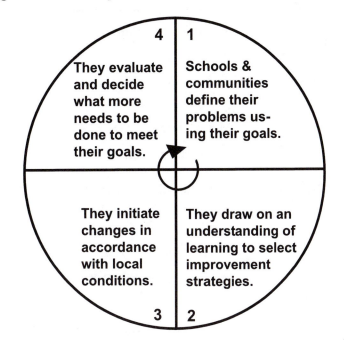

The North Central Regional Educational Laboratory (NCREL) further reports that

> The school improvement cycle involves a team effort. Representatives from the local communities and local schools, including individual administrators and teachers, engage in continuous cycles of improvement. It is a self-regulating cycle—the team decides for itself what its schools should be, how they should operate, and in what ways they should change and improve their approaches to teaching and learning.

Put another way, school improvement includes multiple tasks, as depicted in Figure 1.5 (p. 18).

Figure 1.5. The Processes of School Improvement

Processes of School Improvement	*The Work of School Improvement*
Organizing for School Improvement	♦ Creating a supportive school culture and climate ♦ Promoting teacher leadership ♦ Building teams
Planning for School Improvement	♦ Conducting needs assessments (self-study and gap analysis) to collect and analyze data ♦ Developing goals based on needs ♦ Writing school improvement plans
Implementing School Improvement Plans	♦ Providing the supports needed to achieve school improvement including staff development and supervision ♦ Allocating resources
Monitoring the School Improvement Plan	♦ Conducting gap analysis ♦ Assessing efforts through data ♦ Making modifications ♦ Providing additional resources
Recycling the Process of School Improvement	♦ Repeating the process

The stakes are high for schools and the people involved with them as they work to improve schools. As a construct, the school improvement process is not governed by any universal rules because of the myriad contextual factors found in schools. There are, however, strategies for and approaches to working with teachers and other stakeholders that effective leaders can use to help move the process of school improvement to a more positive end. These are turbulent times for schools and their personnel, with state and federal accountability measures increasing the focus on learning for students, leaders, and the school as an organization. Despite this turbulence, school leaders can take comfort in the work they do to develop strategies to work within their schools toward improvement. Schools and their leaders can accomplish a great deal to ensure the effectiveness of their schools and the programs offered for students and teachers. According to Bruce Hammonds and Wayne Morris of leading-learning. co.nz, there are several factors found in improving and effective schools. These factors can serve as a guide for schools and their personnel as they move forward with the work of school improvement.

Eleven Factors for Effective Schools

1. *Professional Leadership.* This is a key factor in bringing about change. Leaders of effective schools tend to be proactive, participate and share leadership, and have real knowledge of what goes on in the classroom.

2. *Shared Vision and Goals.* Effective schools build consensus on the aims and values of the school and develop a sense of community. This provides a unity of purpose, a consistency of practice, and ownership through collegiality and collaboration.

3. *A Learning Environment.* The shared vision and values determine the ethos of the school. Effective schools have an orderly environment and an attractive working environment, including the display of children's work.

4. *Concentration on Teaching and Learning.* Effectiveness is clearly dependent on effective classroom teaching. It is vital that schools focus on quality as well as the quantity of teaching and learning. Such schools make maximum use of learning time and place an emphasis on mastery of basic skills and the development of an achievement orientation.

5. *Purposeful Teaching.* Quality teaching is at the heart of effective schooling. Such teaching is based on efficient organization with teachers who are clear about their objectives and students who are aware of the purposes, and structured lessons with teachers making use of a range of explicit teaching strategies Teachers use adaptive practice to modify and adapt curriculum material to suit student individual differences.

6. *High Expectations.* Positive high expectations are among of the most important factors. Teachers set high standards to challenges and monitor progress. High expectations also apply to teachers. Teachers convey and reinforce high expectations. Students are encouraged to use their creative imagination and powers of problem solving.

7. *Positive Reinforcement.* This is the most important element of all. This occurs where there is clear and fair discipline and where students feel they belong and are able to participate. Direct and positive feedback has a positive effect with student behavior, and praise needs to be specific, spontaneous, and varied.

8. *Monitoring Progress.* Well-established mechanisms for monitoring the progress of pupils, classes, the school as a whole, and improvement programs are important features. Monitoring by itself has little effect but is an important ingredient in an effective school to determine schoolwide progress. Some schools misdirect teaching through too-frequent monitoring procedures. The key is appropriate monitoring. Evaluating school progress is particularly important.

9. *Pupils' Rights and Responsibilities.* Research indicates that there are considerable gains to be made when pupils' self-esteem is raised and when they have an active role and responsibility for their own learning.

10. *Home–School Partnership.* Supportive relations and cooperation between home and school have positive effects. Effective schools not only involve parents but also make demands on them. The relationship between the individual teacher and the parent(s) is critical.

11. *A Learning Organization.* Effective schools are learning organizations where all aspects of the school are interrelated. To be effective, development needs to be school based and tailored to the specific needs of the school. There is value in embedding staff development within collegial and collaborative planning and ensuring ideas are shared.

Source: http://www.leading-learning.co.nz/school-vision/eleven-factors.html. Used with permission.

Suggested Readings

DuFour, R., & Eaker, R. (1998). *Professional learning communities at work: Best practices for enhancing student achievement.* Bloomington, IN: National Educational Service.

Fielder, D. (2003). *Achievement now! How to assure no child is left behind.* Larchmont, NY: Eye on Education.

Fink, D. (1999). Deadwood didn't kill itself: A pathology of failing schools. *Educational Management & Administration, 27*(2), 131–141.

Fullan, M. (2001). *Leading in a culture of change.* San Francisco: Jossey-Bass.

Harris, A. (2001). Building the capacity for school improvement. *School Leadership and Management, 21*(3), 261–270.

Harris, A. (2002). *School improvement: What's in it for schools?* New York: RoutledgeFalmer.

Harris, A., & Bennett, N. (Eds.). (2001). *School effectiveness and school improvement: Alternative perspectives.* London: Cassell.

Harris, A. (2003). The changing context of leadership: Research, theory, and practice. In A. Harris, C. Day, D. Hopkins, M. Hadfield, A. Hargreaves, & C. Chapman (Eds.), *Effective leadership for school improvement* (pp. 9–25). London: RoutledgeFalmer.

Harris, A., Day, C., Hopkins, D., Hadfield, M., Hargreaves, A., & Chapman, C. (Eds.). (2003). *Effective leadership for school improvement.* London: RoutledgeFalmer.

Lambert, L. (2003). *Leadership capacity for lasting school improvement.* Alexandria, VA: Association for Supervision and Curriculum Development.

Tucker, M. S., & Codding, J. B. (1998). *Standards for our schools: How to set them, measure them, and reach them.* San Francisco: Jossey-Bass.

U.S. Department of Education. (1998). *Turning around low-performing schools: A guide for state and local leaders.* Washington, DC: U.S. Government Printing Office. Author.

2

Principals Promote a Healthy Culture and Climate

In this Chapter...

- ◆ Defining school culture in a context of school improvement
- ◆ Markers of school culture
- ◆ The health of the school culture
- ◆ School climate
- ◆ Two dimensions of climate—Academic and social climate
- ◆ Leadership—Building culture and climate
- ◆ Key norms—Collaboration and trust

Introduction

As instructional leader, the principal must understand the complexities of the school's culture as it "reflects what organizational members care about, what they are willing to spend time doing, what and how they celebrate, and what they talk about" (Robbins & Alvy, 1995, p. 23). Not only do effective instructional leaders understand the school's culture, but they also promote the conditions that foster collaboration, trust, and care that are some of the markers of a healthy and vibrant school culture. School improvement occurs within the context of the school, and this is why it is important to understand the culture and climate of the school.

The school's culture encompasses the school, including the instructional program, the programs offered to students (e.g., athletics and activities), professional development opportunities offered to teachers (e.g., staff development, instructional supervision), the way newcomers are socialized to the school and its community (e.g., mentoring and induction), and the ways in which people interact with one another. Depending on whether positive or negative, the school's culture can be comforting—providing a safety net—or stressful—producing a storm cloud over the work teachers and administrators are trying to accomplish while improving the system. According to Stolp and Smith (1995), "the culture tells people in the school what is truly important and how they are to act" (p. 14). To this end, culture is the bedrock of the organization and worthy of the time and energy needed to understand, promote, and, in some instances, change it (Deal & Peterson, 1999). Culture is a defining point for the school and what occurs in it—when, how, under what circumstances, why, and, in some instances, why not.

Defining School Culture in a Context of School Improvement

Every school has a culture, and whether it is healthy or toxic depends on numerous variables that unfold in the school—the faculty lounge, classrooms, and hallways; private meetings with students, parents, and teachers; sporting events, plays, and assemblies (Deal & Peterson, 1999). Peterson (2002) explains that

> School culture is the set of norms, values and beliefs, rituals and ceremonies, symbols and stories that make up the "persona" of the school. These unwritten expectations build up over time as teachers, administrators, parents, and students work together, solve problems, deal with challenges, and, at times, cope with failures. (p. 10)

In a sense, culture is the sum of the formal and informal behaviors, norms, beliefs, values, and assumptions of the school community, and they influence the ways in which people respond to planning and implementing school improvement (see Chapters 5, 6, and 7).

Cultures are Built on Values, Assumptions, and Norms

The values, assumptions, and norms shape the culture of the school, and they are interrelated (Figure 2.1). It is almost impossible to separate the values, assumptions, and norms from the culture of the school, because they are deeply rooted in history by traditions and rituals and in the day-to-day operations and the communication patterns of the school (Schein, 1996; 1992).

Values are principles, philosophies, beliefs, and ideals that are considered worthwhile to either the person or the group. The school's culture is rooted deeply in values—those principles and ideals that are worthwhile. What is valued is embraced, what is valued is practiced, what is valued is rewarded, and what is valued is perpetuated. Chance and Chance (2002) explain that the underlying values and beliefs of a school are often described in terms of assumptions and norms.

**Figure 2.1. The Interrelated Nature of Values,
Assumptions, and Norms to the School Culture**

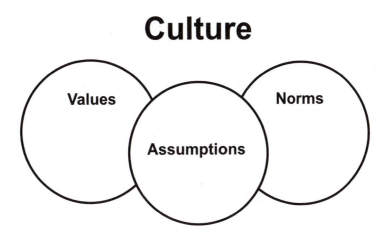

Assumptions are ideas and concepts that are accepted as true and nonnegotiable by the people in the organization. Assumptions are seldom discussed, and they are inherently taken for granted. Assumptions include core beliefs that represent what people believe are right; and assumptions are powerful beliefs that call people to action. *Norms* are "unwritten rules of behavior that arise from cultural assumptions" (Chance & Chance, 2002, p. 21). Norms are important because they help to keep people functioning as a group instead as a collection of people.

Framing Assumptions, Values, and Norms in the Context of School Improvement

A healthy culture can serve to

- Unify people within the school and its many communities.
- Assist with establishing a plan of school improvement.
- Signal an action orientation to get to a plan of school improvement.
- Focus people on the future and point to what the school wants to become.
- Promote growth by providing the means for people to stretch while facing the challenges associated with reaching the many markers of school improvement.

♦ Empower the organization and its people to hold beliefs and values about schooling—the work of teachers, students, and the opportunities each has for developing.

♦ Help schools assess the overall effect of efforts at improvement.

Before school improvement can be approached, members of the school community need to examine the values, beliefs, and assumptions that members embrace. Figure 2.2 can assist the community in bringing to the surface the values, beliefs, and assumptions held by members of the school community. School size should dictate whether this activity occurs at a faculty meeting or in smaller groups, such as grade-level or by department. However, in the end, the values, beliefs, and assumptions identified need to be shared and can serve as one way to get people talking about what they embrace.

Figure 2.2. Identifying Values, Beliefs, and Assumptions

Questions to Ask	*Tracking Responses*
1. Schools should teach…	
2. A good school is one that…	
3. A successful student is able to…	
4. An effective classroom is one in which…	
5. A good school/central office staff member (i.e., teacher, principal, supervisor) is one who…	
6. An effective school faculty/central office division is one that…	
7. A quality instructional program includes…	

Source: Seikaly (2002). *Exercise for Identifying Core Beliefs*. Used with permission. http://www.mdk12.org/process/leading/core_beliefs.html

The values of the principal are central to school improvement. Values, beliefs, and assumptions motivate and they give direction; they focus the principal on what is important and why. Many would agree that success as witnessed in student growth and development can only be achieved with the clear message as manifested in words, deeds, and actions that children can be successful and that they can be reached no matter what. In Chapter 5, an extended case study of the work of Dr. Ruth O'Dell, principal of Lindsey Elementary School (Warner Robins, GA), details what and how she led the school toward improvement, although the school at one time was ranked the lowest-performing school in the county. It was O'Dell's belief that all children can learn and all teachers can teach children how to learn that sustained school improvement at Lindsey Elementary School was possible. Chapman's (2003) work indicates that effective schools have a "an achievement culture where everyone could succeed" (p. 139).

The values of a principal serve as a moral sounding board, and they often reflect what a principal does and how she responds. According to Seikaly (2002), values shape what principals do as leaders, and the principal can influence school improvement by understanding not only the culture of the school but also the personal values that motivate behavior, communication, and actions (e.g., the types of decisions that are made and why). The principal can further clarify values by answering key questions, including the following:

- What does the principal plan for?

- What does the principal monitor?

- What does the principal model?

- What does the principal reinforce through recognition and celebration?

- What behavior is the principal willing to confront?

(See http://www.mdk12.org process/leading/principals_role.html.)

As a reflective practice to help frame the values of the administrative team, the principal might consider leading the administrative team in identifying the collective values of the team by answering and then as a team, coming to an understanding of the following questions:

- As a team, we plan for...

- As a team, we monitor...

- As a team, we model...

- As a team, we recognize and celebrate...

- As a team, we will are willing to confront...

The answers to these questions should serve as a guide not only for managing the day-to-day operations of the school, but also for leading the school in its improvement efforts. To be effective, administrative team members need to be on the same proverbial page; otherwise, teachers, students, and others can be confounded by mixed messages.

Putting Culture into Context— Using Metaphor to Express Culture

One way to think about school culture is to think about metaphors. A metaphor is a tool used to convey that an image X is equal to Y to make a comparison between the two objects. The meaning derived from the metaphor is found in the comparison. Consider how the following metaphors give a visual picture of the school. Think about the possible values of a school that portrays itself as a puzzle palace or a flagship.

Metaphor	X is equal to Y
My school is like a puzzle palace.	School is equal to a puzzle palace
This school is a sleeping giant.	School is equal to a sleeping giant
Within our district, our school is the jewel in the crown.	School is equal to a jewel in the crown.
We are the flagship middle school.	We are equal to a flagship middle school.

Of course, in a literal sense a school is not a puzzle palace, a sleeping giant, a jewel in the crown, or a flagship. However, each one of these metaphors conveys beliefs and values—the cultural representation of a school. Metaphors help people make sense of their situation; metaphors provide a mental picture of a reality held to be true. Take a few minutes, and examine the mission statement of your school. Identify and examine the values inherent in the mission statement. Now, develop a metaphor that captures the values and the culture of your school. Figure 2.3 can assist with tracking the metaphors that express the culture of the school.

Figure 2.3. Tracking Metaphors to Describe School Culture

Mission Statement	Values	Metaphor(s)
		Meanings of the Metaphor

This activity might be worthwhile to conduct at a faculty meeting or with smaller groups (e.g., grade levels and departments) to get people to examine their perspectives about culture and the meanings related to the culture that the school community attaches to the metaphors. As follow-up activity, the faculty should revisit the metaphors to see if, how, and why cultural metaphors change over time.

Formal and Informal Cultures and Subcultures

Identifying school culture is a complex undertaking and cannot be reduced to merely having members of the community list their beliefs, values, and assumptions, because a school, like any other organization, has both a *formal* and an *informal* culture. Moreover, within any given culture there are *subcultures* that can complement or detract from the work of the mainstream culture.

Think about the value "all children will be treated fairly" as indicated in the school mission statement. This value resonates with most people; however, think about a scenario in which a large number of students are served by free and reduced lunches and in which a particular grade level has a practice where students who do not bring two rolls of paper towels cannot use art supplies. It is probably safe to assume given the population of the school (e.g., poverty) that the actions of the teachers on this team are not in sync with the value of fairness.

The formal aspects of culture include, for example, job descriptions, traditions that people uphold, and the values and ideals in the mission statement. Some aspects of the formal culture are barely noticeable because everyone knows these aspects. They are taken for granted, and they are based on history that is passed on from year-to-year by the members of the school. The formal aspects of the school's culture are defined by symbols (e.g., the school mascot), the school song, and other artifacts that help to define the culture as "what it is."

The informal aspects of culture include, for example, how people interact with one another and share information, and how work gets accomplished and by whom. The informal aspects of culture are fuzzy, in that people do what they always do not necessarily because *this* or *that* is in a job description or a rule, but because that is "just the way things get done."

The larger the school, the more likely there will be subcultures. The very structure of divisions in schools by teams, departments, and grade levels lead to the formation of subcultures in the school. Subcultures can exist formally—for example, grade levels—or informally—people who share a particular set of beliefs or values and who resonate as a smaller group of the whole school community. Subcultures may or may not share the same values, assumptions, and norms as the primary culture.

When differences in values, assumptions, and norms between the primary culture and subcultures emerge, conflict might occur in which the focus of school improvement efforts can be sidetracked. Effective leaders listen to and acknowledge the perspectives of subcultures regardless of whether these views and voices resonate with the efforts of the school and its work with school improvement. Each school context is different, and these differences should dictate how the principal responds to subcultures. It is important to consider the possible contributions that dissenting points of view can have in the school improvement process.

Markers of School Culture

School cultures are as individual as the site in which they evolve, and culture is everywhere. A school's culture rests squarely on "a dominant and coherent set of shared values conveyed by symbolic means such as stories, myths, legends, slogans, anecdotes, and fairy tales" (Peters & Waterman, 1982, p. 103). Effective principals are not only able to identify markers of a school's culture, but they are also, and perhaps more importantly, "capable of assessing, building, and brokering effective school cultures—[and this] is necessary if principals are to continue to enhance their roles as effective agents of school improvement" (pp. 85–86). The assessment of the school's culture cannot occur until the markers—the stuff that culture is made of—are identified.

Markers of a school's culture include the mission statement, student programs, programs for teachers, and the physical plant. Although not exhaustive, the following will take you in the direction of discovering the values, beliefs, and attitudes—all that encompasses the school culture. Principals identify the markers of a school's culture in a variety of ways, including walking around; examining documents; talking with internal and external stakeholders; and observing people, rituals, and customs while participating in school events.

Mission Statement and Other Documents

The school's mission statement is a cultural representation of the school, and building a strong mission relates directly to the culture of the school. By examining the mission statement and other documents, the principal can examine the school's culture. Figure 2.4 shows a guide for the examination of school culture, as related to the mission statement and other documents. The principal is encouraged to consider other documents that are particular to the context of the school.

Figure 2.4. Examining the Mission Statement and Other Documents

Mission Statement

- What are the ideas and ideals promoted in the mission statement?

- What values are communicated about students? Teachers?

- When was the mission statement written?

- Who was involved in writing this document?

- Is the document still timely, given the context of the school, the characteristics of the student body, and the community that the school serves?

- What academic programs promote these ideas and ideals?

- What other available documents give clues about the school's mission and philosophy?

- What messages do these documents give to teachers, students, and faculty?

- How is the mission statement or school philosophy referenced in these documents?

Other Documents

Documents can include student and teacher handbooks, the school newspaper and yearbook, program descriptions, curriculum guides, letters to parents, school report cards, and any other words that are printed by or about the school.

- Examine programs (academic/curricular, athletic, and social). Do these programs reach out to students and parents to meet the mission? (Look at, for example, the honors program, special needs programs for at-risk students, and the guidance program.)

- Examine the school song and cheers. Are there unifying messages in each? Are the messages consistent with the school's mission statement and philosophy?

- Examine school colors, mascot, and logo. Do these items reinforce the identity of the school relative to the mission statement and philosophy?

- Do students proudly wear coats, jackets, T-shirts, and other clothing items with the school's logo and colors?

- Are students proud to be part of the school community?

Source: Adapted from Calabrese, Short, & Zepeda (1996). Used with permission.

Policy Statements

All schools have policies and procedures to enact them. Policies give direction, provide a blueprint for organization, and ensure equitable treatment. Clues about a school's culture can be found in policies, but perhaps, more importantly, the procedures that ensure that policies are enacted give a clearer understanding of the school's culture. Consider both policies and procedures when examining the school's culture (Figure 2.5).

Figure 2.5. Policy Statements and School Culture

Policy Statements

♦ Are policies readily available to faculty? When new policies are enacted at either the central office level or the site level, are teachers provided explanations about them?

♦ At the site level, do teachers engage in developing policies and give input on how to establish procedures to meet the spirit of policies?

♦ Are policies communicated to parents, students, and other stakeholders?

♦ Are policies assessed to determine their desired effects?

♦ Are policies developed only when necessary? If there are too many policies, then stakeholders will feel cornered by an overabundance of rules and regulations.

♦ Are policies upheld fairly, consistently, and equitably among groups within the school?

♦ Are policies used as a way to encourage discussion versus as a means to get a closed answer?

Programs for Students

The principal is responsible for the overall academic program, including programs for students such as activities, special education, a recognition plan, and guidance program, to name a few. Students are the reason why schools exist. To enhance program development, principals must understand the programs, including their rationale, goals, and standards by which they are judged, and the contemporary issues that surround them (Figure 2.6). The types of programs offered, the staffing of these programs, and the (fiscal) priority programs are given in the overall mix of the school refer back to the culture of the school and answer the question, what do people value?

Figure 2.6. Programs that Shape the School Culture

Programs for Students

The Types of Support Programs Available for Students

♦ What programs are available for students?

♦ Do these programs match student needs?

♦ Do these programs continually seek the perspectives of teachers, parents, guidance counselors, central office administrators, and students in the development and design of them?

♦ Given what you discover, do programs need to be modified, eliminated, or added?

♦ Do the policies of the *discipline plan* promote the beliefs of the mission statement?

♦ What policies are inconsistent with the mission statement?

Types of Student Recognition Programs—What Is Recognized?

♦ Who is recognized and when are they recognized?

♦ Is there equity and equality in student recognition programs?

Types of Schoolwide Celebrations—What Gets Celebrated?

♦ How?

♦ When?

♦ Who is involved with the celebrations?

Effective Discipline Plans

*(U.S. Department of Education,
http://www.ed.gov/offices/OSERS/OSEP/earlywrn.html)*

♦ Focus on academic achievement.

♦ Develop links to the community.

♦ Emphasize positive relationships among students and staff.

♦ Discuss safety issues openly.

♦ Treat students with equal respect.

♦ Create ways for students to share their concerns.

♦ Help children feel safe expressing their feelings.

♦ Have in place a system for referring children who are suspected of being abused or neglected.

♦ Offer extended-day programs for children.

♦ Promote good citizenship and character.

♦ Identify problems and assess progress toward solutions.

♦ Support students in making the transition to adult life and the workplace.

Sources: Adapted from Calabrese, Short, & Zepeda (1996). Used with permission. U.S. Department of Education (1998). *Early Warning, Timely Response:* A Guide to Safe Schools. http://cecp.air.org/guide/guide.pdf.

Programs for Teachers

An important aspect of understanding the culture of a school is to know the faculty and the types of learning opportunities available to them vis-à-vis staff development, supervision, leadership opportunities, workplace conditions, and the relationships that teachers have with each other and the administration (Figure 2.7).

Figure 2.7. Programs for Teachers that Shape the School Culture

Programs for Teachers

♦ What types of professional development activities are available for teachers?

♦ How many teachers participate in these activities?

♦ What types of programs would teachers like to see initiated?

♦ What types of leadership activities are available for teachers?

♦ How many teachers are involved in formal and informal leadership activities?

♦ What types of teacher recognition programs are in place?

Professional Development...
(U.S. Department of Education (1995))

♦ Focuses on teachers as central to student learning, yet includes all members of the school community.

♦ Focuses on individual, collegial, and organizational improvement.

♦ Respects and nurtures the intellectual and leadership capacity of teachers, principals, and others in the school community.

♦ Reflects the best available research and practice in teaching, learning, and leadership.

♦ Enables teachers to develop further expertise in subject content, teaching strategies, uses of technologies, and other essential elements of teaching to high standards.

♦ Promotes continuous inquiry and improvement embedded in the daily life of schools.

♦ Is planned collaboratively by those who will participate in and facilitate that development;

♦ Requires substantial time and resources.

♦ Is driven by a coherent long-term plan.

♦ Is evaluated ultimately on the basis of its effects on teacher instruction and student learning, and uses this assessment to guide subsequent professional development efforts.

Sources: Adapted from Calabrese, Short, & Zepeda (1996). Used with permission. U.S. Department of Education (1995). *Building Bridges: The Mission and Principles of Professional Development.* http://www.ed.gov/G2K/bridge.html.

The Learning Environment

The learning environment includes the physical plant—commons, hallways, gymnasium, faculty lounge, library, classrooms—and anywhere else people convene—playground, parking lot. The physical environment gives clues about what people value, and the condition of the learning environment also makes a statement to those who work in them. Duke (quoted in Stanton, 1999) states that "physical entities like a school come to symbolize certain qualities, values, aspirations, and experiences for individuals," and Stanton reports that there is

> anecdotal evidence linking student achievement—as well as behavior—to the physical conditions and overcrowding of school buildings. Good facilities are an important precondition for learning, provided other conditions are present that support a strong academic program in the school. Likewise, adverse environmental conditions—such as crumbling plaster, poor lighting, inadequate ventilation, and inoperative heating and cooling systems—can affect learning negatively, as well as the health and morale of staff and students.

Examine the elements presented in Figure 2.8 (p. 36) to determine the quality of the learning environment in your school.

The Health of the School Culture

At far ends of a continuum, a school's culture can be healthy and vibrant, or it can be toxic, marked with dysfunctional patterns of behavior (Peterson, 2002). Toxic cultures deplete energy, damage its members, and make it nearly impossible to work toward the collaborative means needed to shepherd school improvement efforts because "the elements of culture reinforce negativity. Values and beliefs are negative. The cultural network works in opposition to anything positive. Rituals and traditions are phony, joyless, or counterproductive" (Deal & Peterson, 1999, p. 119). Deal and Peterson report that toxic cultures evolve "over time," and that in schools that are toxic, "staffs are extremely fragmented,…the purpose of students has been lost to the goal of serving adults, where negative values and hopelessness reigns" (p. 28). Toxic schools create a wasteland for students, teachers, and others—both internal and external constituents.

At the other end of the continuum is a healthy school culture that has the conditions that support "desirable cultural characteristic of schools as they face what are now the new norms of high-stakes testing and the attendant accountability for learning outcomes" (Leonard, 2002, p. 1). Leonard indicates that more positive cultures are marked by professional collaboration that is "evidenced when teachers and administrators, share their knowledge, contribute

Figure 2.8. The Aspects of the Learning Environment that Shape the School Culture

The Learning Environment

♦ What is the general condition of the school's interior? Do the walls need to be painted? Are the walls kept clean from graffiti?

♦ Are there windows for natural light within the classrooms?

♦ Do supervisable circulation patterns exist (giving students a sense of freedom)?

♦ Air quality: Is the HVAC system capable of exchanging air at the standard rate of 15 cubic feet per minute per person (American Society of Heating, Refrigeration, and Air-Conditioning Engineering)?

♦ Wall coloring: Are classroom walls painted in soft tones to keep the students calm, with brighter colors for emphasis on certain pathways (halls, promenades)?

♦ Do gymnasiums, playing fields, the auditorium or theater, and entryways display markers of the school's culture?

♦ Does the school have an *outdoor* classroom (in addition to football stadiums, baseball fields, and gymnasiums)?

♦ Are driveways and parking lots clear of clutter and maintained?

♦ Is the school's surrounding landscape neatly kept? Lined with trees, scrubs, flowers?

♦ Do student-made artifacts grace the walls in the hallways, foyers, and bulletin boards? Are there student designed murals depicting the history of their school?

♦ Are trophies displayed in cases throughout the school (including academic achievement)?

♦ Are press releases related to events at the school posted in a central place where students can read about the events and accomplishments of students and teachers?

♦ Are classrooms decorated and neatly kept?

♦ Is the cafeteria relaxing and conducive to a peaceful eating period?

♦ Are the bathrooms smoke-free and safe?

♦ Is the carpeting routinely maintained? Windows cleaned?

Sources: Adapted from Tanner (2002). Used with permission.

ideas, and develop plans for the purpose of achieving educational and organizational goals" (p. 4). In healthy school cultures, principals work with teachers—they have a shared vision and mission, they focus on student learning, and they work under a common set of assumptions about learning for both students and adults.

A positive culture is *aligned*, and goals and objectives are consistent with the mission. A positive culture fosters genuine collegiality. In a healthy culture, empowerment is the norm among students and teachers, teacher and administrators, and parents and teachers and administrators.

School Climate

School culture and climate are "often intertwined and are both related to organizational behavior and productivity" (Fiore, 2001, p. 8). Halpin and Croft (1963) provide an analogy that can assist with understanding the broad construct of school climate: "Personality is to the individual what climate is to the organization" (p. 1). School climate is the social atmosphere in which people interact with others and the school environment.

School climate includes the perceptions that people have of various aspects of the internal environment (safety; high expectations; relationships with teachers, students, parents, and administrators). Moreover, school climate includes the aspects of the school that influence behavior—how people interact with one another:

> The elements that make up school climate are complex, ranging from the quality of interactions in the teachers' lounge to the noise levels in hallways and cafeterias, from the physical structure of the building to the physical comfort levels (involving such factors as heating, cooling, and lighting) of the individuals and how safe they feel. Even the size of the school and the opportunities for students and teachers to interact in small groups both formally and informally add to or detract from the health of the learning environment. (Freiberg, 1998, p. 22)

Figure 2.9 (p. 38) offers an overview of the factors that assist in the development and maintenance of a positive school climate.

Figure 2.9. The Development and Maintenance of a Positive School Climate

Positive School Climates are Enhanced When the Following Exist:

♦ A clear school mission, which promotes student achievement

♦ Well-established expectations for success

♦ Consistently delivered quality classroom instruction

♦ Effective communication among all members of the school with a special focus on feedback to parents and students

♦ Strong morale

♦ Maintenance of a safe, well-ordered learning environment

♦ Demonstrated effective instructional leadership

♦ Balanced interaction between students and teachers

♦ Clearly, communicated expectations for student behavior, which are consistently enforced and fairly applied

Source: Government of Newfoundland and Labrador, Department of Education and Student Support Services (1995). *Positive School Climate*. http://www.edu.gov.nf.ca/ discipline/pos_schl_clim.htm

An examination of Fiore's (2001) physical representation of the intertwined nature of climate and culture is worthy to examine, and this representation (Figure 2.10) shows that "school culture is the supporting structure on which the school climate rests" (p. 18).

Figure 2.10. Iceberg Analogy to Portray Culture and Climate

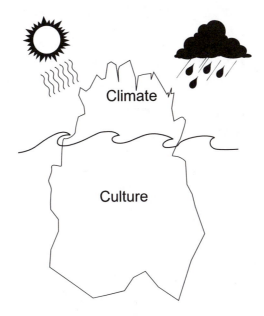

Source: Fiore (2001). Used with permission.

Two Dimensions of Climate— Academic and Social Climate

Sackney (1988) believes there are two distinct dimensions of a school's climate—the academic climate and the social climate, and he offers the following description of the academic and social climates found in schools.

> The *academic climate* is a resultant of how the school uses rewards and praise, the effectiveness of the teachers and the principal, and the collaborative processes that exist within the school. The *social climate*, on the other hand, is a resultant of the appearance, comfort, and orderliness of the school facility, the opportunities students have for participation in the school program, the peer norms that are prevalent, and the nature of the administrative staff-student cohesion and support systems. Taken together, the dimensions and attributes contribute to a positive school climate.

According to Sackney (1988), there are two dimensions that build a school's climate, and these dimensions are presented in Figure 2.11(p. 40). Each one of the dimensions includes attributes that work in tandem and, when examined in their totality, gives an approach to develop a picture of the health of the school climate (positive or negative).

Figure 2.11. Academic and Social Climate

Source: Sackney (1988). *Attributes of a positive school climate. Enhancing school learn-ing climate: Theory, research, and practice.* Used with permission. http://www.ssta.sk.ca/research/school_improvement/180.htm.

Leadership— Building Culture and Climate

Healthy cultures and positive climates do not magically occur. Strong cultures emerge, in part, by the efforts of the principal to support and nurture people, connect and align people and programs, launch a vision rooted in the belief that all children can learn, and empower teachers, all while building a learning community supportive of improvement.

Whatever the principal and administrative team model will profoundly shape the culture and the practices that, in turn, further serve to shape and to mold the culture. There is nothing more visible than the work of the principal, and what the principal and the members of the administrative team emphasize, reward, and sanction come to symbolize publicly what is important. Fiore (2001) believes that there are key behaviors of principals in schools that reinforce healthy or unhealthy cultures (Figure 2.12).

Figure 2.12. Principal Behaviors: Healthy and Unhealthy Cultures

Principals in Healthy Cultures...	*Principals in Unhealthy Cultures...*
◆ Are visible to all stakeholders.	◆ Are rarely seen outside their office.
◆ Communicate regularly and purposefully.	◆ Find little time for communication.
◆ Never forget that they are role models.	◆ Feel that other people are responsible for their school building's physical needs—they take passive roles in decorating and furnishing their schools.
◆ Are passionate about their work.	
◆ Accept responsibility for the school's culture.	
◆ Are organized.	◆ See themselves as the lone leader or "boss" of the school—they never empower teachers to lead.
◆ Exhibit a positive outlook.	
◆ Take pride in the physical environment of the school.	◆ Are poorly organized.
◆ Empower others appropriately.	◆ Habitually make excuses for their school's shortcomings, blaming inadequacies on outside influences.
◆ Demonstrate stewardship—they protect their school and its people.	

Source: Fiore (2001). Principal Behaviors—Healthy and Unhealthy Cultures. Used with permission.

Figure 2.13 (p. 42) further amplifies the relationship between culture and the leadership of the principal.

Figure 2.13. School Culture and Principal Leadership

Organization Leadership Types	Leadership Behaviors	Aspects of Culture and Climate

Type A
 	
Transactional Leadership
	◆ Top-down decisions
	
	◆ Transactional approach: Leaders set the goals, communicate the goals, and reward those who meet the goals.
	
	◆ Rules
	
	◆ Positional power
		◆ Closed climate
		
		◆ Toxic cultures:
		  1. Lack a clear sense of purpose
		  2. Have norms that reinforce inertia
		  3. Blame students for lack of progress
		  4. Discourage collaboration
		  5. Often have actively hostile relations among staff
		◆ Teachers are engaged in trivial busywork.

Type Z
 	
Transformational Leadership
	◆ Collaborative decisions
	
	◆ Transformational approach: Leaders engage others in collaborative goal setting, decision making, planning, and evaluating.
	
	◆ Collaboration is the norm
		◆ Open climate
		
		◆ In healthy cultures:
		  1. Communication flows openly among teachers, students, and administrators
		  2. High levels of commitment to the work of student success from teachers
		  3. Leadership is not restrictive but rather supportive of teachers, respectful of teacher competence.
		  4. Adaptable
		◆ Teachers are engaged in purposeful work marked by creativity.

Sources: Adapted from Chance & Chance (2002); Deal & Peterson (1999); Cromwell (2002); Leithwood (1992); Peterson (2002).

The leadership of the principal is critically important in the development of a healthy culture. Building a healthy school culture is a multifaceted, complex undertaking; unfortunately, there are no absolutes. However, there are certain conditions that principals can strive to provide to build and sustain a culture to build a healthy school climate. The efforts of the principal must be pervasive—shortcuts will dilute the efforts and signal insincerity to commitment for the vision of what schools need to strive toward school improvement. The principal must sustain a culture that focuses the efforts of teachers and others to influence the direction of school improvement. School cultures that support the norms of collaboration and trust yield better results.

Key Norms: Collaboration and Trust

Healthy school cultures and climates thrive in environments built through collaboration, trust, and care for the members of the school. Although the final responsibility for school improvement falls to the principal, building culture can never be built through the sole efforts of the principal, as Lane (1992) vigorously asserts:

> The culture-building mode is not meant to imply that the principal single-handedly constructs the school culture. Rather, it is meant to describe the principal's efforts to influence or shape the existing values and norms of the culture in a direction that best supports instructional effectiveness. (p. 92)

Characteristics of Collaborative Cultures

Kruse, Louis, and Bryk (1994, pp. 4–5) identify the following characteristics of collaborative school cultures:

- ♦ Critical elements of school communities: reflective dialogue, deprivatization of practice, collective focus on student learning, collaboration, and shared norms and values.

- ♦ Structural conditions: time to meet and talk, physical proximity, interdependent teaching roles, communications structures, and teacher empowerment.

- ♦ Social and human factors: openness to improvement, trust and respect, cognitive and skill-based teaching and learning, supportive leadership, and socialization of teachers.

The principal is in a position to support the development of each of these conditions through a variety of means that range from shared decision making to implementing peer-coaching programs, and from supporting beginning teachers through formal and informal mentoring programs to providing time for teachers to meet.

Building Collaborative School Cultures

Building collaborative school cultures and positive school climates is dependent on several variables including, most notably, norms and workplace conditions. These conditions are interrelated, and together they form both the culture and climate of the school.

Norms

Norms are unwritten rules of behavior that serve as a guide to the way people interact with one another (Chance & Chance, 2002). Saphier and King (1985) identify 12 norms of school culture, which, if strong, contribute to the instructional effectiveness of a school:

- *Collegiality:* People interact with one another, the members of the community are open and to one another.

- *Experimentation:* Risk taking is encouraged.

- *High expectations:* People have high expectations for themselves, for each other, and for students.

- *Trust and confidence:* People trust one another.

- *Tangible support:* Resources—time, support—are present.

- *Reaching out to the knowledge bases:* Information is available.

- *Appreciation and recognition:* People feel important and respected and like they are part of the school. They feel that what they do is important, and that colleagues, administrators, and the larger community hold the work they accomplish in high esteem.

- *Caring, celebration, and humor:* People thrive when they feel emotionally supported. Communities take the time to celebrate—the big and small accomplishments of each other and students.

- *Involvement in decision making:* Decision making spans the school environment and is not just a function of the administration.

- *Protection of what is important:* Principals and others identify what is important and then protect time and secure resources to support priorities.

- *Traditions:* Traditions shape the culture, and traditions are upheld as part of the community.

- *Honest, open communication:* People talk to one another; they share ideas openly without fear.

Collegiality and Collaboration

Principals interested in school improvement and fostering the conditions for school improvement promote collegial and collaborative relationships among teachers. The school climate dictates whether or not teachers collaborate with one another and whether or not interactions are collegial and inviting. Barth (1990) suggests that a number of positive outcomes may be associated with collegiality, namely, the development and implementation of better decisions, increased levels of adult and student motivation to learn, and conditions that "sustain all other attempts at school improvement" (p. 31). Similarly, Hargreaves (1997) reports that

> Cultures of collaboration among teachers seem to produce greater willingness to take risks, to learn from mistakes, and share successful strategies with colleagues that lead to teachers having positive senses of their own efficiency, beliefs that their children can learn, and improved outcomes....(p. 68)

However, there can be a dark side to collegiality, and according to Hargreaves (1997), "Contrived collegiality does not so much deceive teachers as delay, distract, and demean them" (p. 73) because the very characteristics of contrived collegiality are

- administratively regulated...that requires teachers to meet and work together;

- compulsory [that] makes working together a matter of compulsion as in mandatory team teaching, peer coaching or collaborative planning;

- implementation–oriented...[that] requires or 'persuades' teachers to work together so as to implement other people's mandates...;

- fixed in time in space...that are administratively determined by others, and,

- predictable...[that] is designed to bring about relatively predictable outcomes. (Hargreaves, p. 73)

Collaboration in schools has been identified as the "key schooling process variable for increasing the norms of student achievement" (Lunenburg, 1995, p. 41). Collaboration is about altering relationships and "is a powerful means of significant and lasting personal growth that may...lead to substantial organizational change" (Christenson, Eldredge, Ibom, Johnston, & Thomas, 1996, p. 187). Collaboration is dependent on the feeling of interdependence (we are in this together) and opportunity. When teachers collaborate, they share ideas and problem-solve solutions to the thorny issues they face in the classroom.

Through collaboration, teachers are able to support growth and development while improving their practices. Collaboration includes such activities as coplanning and teaching lessons, brainstorming ideas, conducting action research, and interclassroom observations (peer coaching), and the reflection and dialogue that follows in post-observation conferences. To break the patterns and norm of isolation prevalent among teachers, time and the commitment of the principal are needed.

Kruse and Louis (1995) report that in cultures that support collaboration, "teachers feel encouraged to work together to develop shared understandings of students, curriculum, and policy, to produce materials and activities that improve instruction and assessment, and to revamp staff development" (p. 2). Collaborative cultures send strong messages to teachers about the seriousness of their work, and students are the beneficiaries of collaborative cultures—teachers working toward the betterment of instructional practices.

Trust

Trust is a prerequisite for building a positive school climate and culture. Without trust, efforts to build a collaborative culture marked by collegial interactions between teachers and administrators will be diminished. Without trust, relationships will flounder. Trust and respect build a strong foundation for the work and efforts of teachers. Without trust, efforts at school improvement will yield few lasting results, and Goodlad (1984) reports that "a bond of trust and mutual support between principal and teachers…appears to be basic to school improvement" (p. 9).

Bryk and Schneider (2002) identify "relational trust" as the core ingredient for school improvement. Relational trust rests on a foundation of respect, competence, personal regard, and integrity. Building and maintaining trust evolves over time. Trust is built on history—the history of trust in the organization and the history of trust between teachers and administrators. A leader must ask several questions:

◆ Do teachers trust me?

◆ Do teachers have confidence in my actions?

◆ Do my words and actions align with each other?

◆ Do teachers believe I hold them in high regard?

◆ Do I exhibit integrity in the way I make decisions, communicate expectations, and allocate resources?

The answers to these questions can serve as a guide to self-discovery about the patterns of trust, and the work needed to build more trusting relationships with teachers. If any of these answers are negative, indicating that trust is an issue, then the principal will need to develop strategy to ensure that words and deeds point to developing and maintaining trust. Because of the change and risk involved in school improvement, teachers need leadership from the principal that fosters trust. Without trust, positive relationships with teachers as well as a willingness to take risks will not be forthcoming.

Caring Builds Trust

With the complex nature of schools, relationships that build interdependence with others are essential to build collaborative cultures. In schools with positive cultures, trust acts as the glue that helps teachers take risks needed to make changes—both in and out of the classroom—and to work together as teams (Peterson, 1999). Trust is built on relationships in which all member of the school are encouraged to contribute, to learn, and to be part of the discussion about school improvement. Trusting relationships thrive in a school culture that embraces two-way communication, feedback, and "care," which includes two primary goals—"promoting human development and responding to needs" (Beck, 1992, pp. 456–457).

Principals, who promote a positive and caring culture, act a certain way that signals to teachers and students that they are able to:

- Achieve more.
- Make decisions because they are empowered.
- Overcome obstacles, view failure as a learning experience.
- Develop their individual and collective strengths.
- Learn from one another and assume greater authority to take on leadership.
- Seek assistance, take risks, and assume responsibility.

Suggested Readings

Bryk, A. S., & Schneider, B. (2002). *Trust in schools: A core resource for improvement.* New York: Russell Sage.

Deal, T. E., & Peterson, K. D. (1999). *Shaping school culture: The heart of leadership.* San Francisco: Jossey-Bass.

Fiore, D. J. (2001). *Creating connections for better schools: How leaders enhance school culture.* Larchmont, NY: Eye on Education.

Freiberg, J. (1998). Measuring school culture. *Educational Leadership, 56*(1), 22–26.

Schein, E. H. (1992). *Organizational Culture and Leadership (2nd ed.).* San Francisco: Jossey-Bass.

Stolp, S., & Smith, S. C. (1995). *Transforming school culture: Stories, symbols, values, and the leader's role.* Eugene, OR: ERIC Clearinghouse on Educational Management, University of Oregon.

3

Principals Support Teacher Leadership

In this Chapter…

- The need for teacher leadership
- A starting point for teacher leadership—scanning the environment
- Cultivating teacher leadership

Introducing Teacher Leadership

Given the complexities of schools and the immense work of school improvement, leadership cannot be vested solely in the principal, and as the saying goes, *No man stands alone*. Principals assert their effectiveness by diffusing leadership to a larger set of stakeholders, that is, teachers. Teachers are among the many variables that will greatly influence school improvement, and Frost and Durrant (2002) conclude from their research "that the nurturing of teachers as leaders is fundamental to effective school improvement. The development of teachers' leadership skills, the exponential growth in confidence and self-esteem, and the release of creative energy have a powerful effect" (p. 157).

Promoting and developing authentic teacher leadership is related to building capacity for both the individual and the organization (Frost & Durrant, 2002; Harris, 2002; Lambert, 2003). Diffusing leadership that builds capacity is much different from delegating work and duties just to get things done or to lighten the workload. Diffusing requires an advocacy for extending the boundaries of authority beyond the position and the person who holds the title, whether principal or administrator.

Promoting and sustaining teacher leadership opportunities will not magically occur; it takes sustained effort. The principal (and other administrators), teachers, and organizational structure of the school must be ready to support teacher leadership. Supporting and nurturing leadership across the school can help to make the work of school improvement more meaningful.

49

The Need for Teacher Leadership

Teacher leadership is important, given what school systems need to do to promote student learning. Schools need teacher leaders to provide leadership and to sustain a strong instructional program for students, and as Bernauer asserts, "any reasonable hope of sustaining a focus on improvement requires full realization of the critical role of teacher leader(s)" (p. 90). "Indeed, if schools are going to become places in which all children are learning, all teachers *must* lead" (Barth, 2001a, p. 444, emphasis in original). Furthering this point, Barth believes a "powerful relationship exists between learning and leading," and that "only when teachers learn will their students learn" (p. 445). Similarly, in a synthesis of the waves of teacher leadership, Silva, Gimbert, and Nolan (2000) conclude that

> teacher leaders would "slide the doors open" to collaborate with other teachers, discuss common problems, share approaches to various learning situations, explore ways to overcome the structural constraints of limited time, space, resources, and restrictive policies, or investigate motivational strategies to bring students to a deeper engagement with their learning. (p. 781)

Teacher leaders promote learning when they lead, and this is why principals must find opportunities for teachers to be involved in leadership within the school and beyond. According to Short and Greer (1997, p. 183), principals who promote leadership

- Build trust.
- Communicate more openly.
- Promote risk taking.
- Engage in open problem solving.
- Build a commitment and support for change.

These are the essential skills that principals need to promote teacher leadership that goes beyond "getting work done" in the school. Effective instructional leaders are able to frame teacher leadership within the context of the school, and they are able to value teachers as leaders who can

- Develop the instructional program.
- Make positive changes in the school.
- Share their expertise with others.
- Shape the culture of the school.

Although discussed separately, this work is interrelated and is essential to framing overall schoolwide improvement.

Teachers as Leaders Develop the Instructional Program

The instructional program in any given school, regardless of level (elementary, middle, high), is complex with regard to the curriculum—content standards, what is to be taught, the pace in which the *what* is taught, and the myriad adaptations that need to be made to the curriculum due, in part, to the needs of students. An examination of instructional artifacts would yield a robust find including textbooks, curriculum and pacing guides, assessment plans, course descriptions, and myriad other documents. As leaders, teachers assume daily the responsibility for ensuring that instruction unfolds in classrooms, and they assume responsibility for what is taught and how. According to Barth (2001a), teachers who are leaders help to shape the culture of the school when they are involved in

- choosing textbooks and instructional materials;
- shaping the curriculum;
- setting standards for student behavior;
- deciding whether students are tracked into special classes;
- designing staff development and inservice programs;
- setting promotion and retention policies;
- deciding school budgets;
- evaluating teacher performance;
- selecting new teachers; and
- selecting new administrators. (p. 444)

The value of the work of teacher leaders in developing the instructional program is in the interactions that teachers have with one another, across and within grade levels, and with central office personnel. Teacher leaders who actively work within the realm of the instructional program often make significant contributions to other related areas beyond their individual classrooms (e.g., staff development needed to assist teachers hone the craft of teaching, development of assessments that are closely related to what is taught).

Teachers as Leaders Make Positive Changes in the School

Teachers who assume leadership beyond the confines of their own classrooms are in a position to emerge as change agents, and according to Chenoweth and Everhart (2002), who credit Sergiovanni (1995) for coining the term *leadership density,*

Leadership density is a key ingredient to strengthening, sustaining, and widely investing participants in the renewal of their schools. With it, we can help ensure that school improvement takes hold and persists in spite of unpredictable personnel changes and numerous environmental challenges. (p. 17)

By diffusing leadership, instructional leaders engage teachers as the actors of change instead of recipients or receivers of change mandated from the top. In schools where teachers are empowered, they emerge as change agents. Why is it important for teachers to be the key actors in implementing change leading to school improvement? Mendez-Morse (1992) cites Nickse (1977), who believes that teachers have credibility to lead as change agents because

- *Teachers have a vested interest:* "They care about what they do and how they do it and feel a sense of responsibility for their efforts."

- *Teachers have a sense of history:* They are "aware of the norms of their colleagues."

- *Teachers know the community:* They "have information concerning the values and attitudes of the community."

- *Teachers can implement change:* They "are where the action is . . . in the position to initiate planned change on the basis of need." (p. 19)

Effective instructional leaders involve teachers in change:

Many people within a school, district, or community possess the needed skills to help provide direction to the change effort. The secret (if there is one) is identifying those skill sets, locating the individuals who can best provide them, and involving them as equal partners. (Chenoweth & Everhart, 2002, p. 7)

Teachers as Leaders Share Their Expertise with Others

Research and practice reveals that one of the most important factors influencing student learning is teacher expertise (Wise & Liebbrand, 1996). Principals who want to enact positive school for lasting school improvement and change recognize and value the expertise that teachers have to offer. Part of this recognition includes the view that expertise involves entrusting teachers to work at continually developing and refining practices that lead to enhanced learning for both teachers and students. In *What Matters Most: Teaching for America's Future*, the National Commission on Teaching & America's Future (1996, p. 10) makes three strong assertions:

1. What teachers know and can do is the most important influence on what students learn.

2. Recruiting, preparing, and retaining good teachers is the central strategy for improving our schools.

3. School reform cannot succeed unless it focuses on creating the conditions in which teachers can teach, and teach well.

In the follow-up report, *Doing What Matters Most: Investing in Quality Teaching*. Darling-Hammond (1997) indicates that

> Teacher expertise—what teachers know and can do—affects all the core tasks of teaching. What teachers understand about content and students shapes how judiciously they select from texts and other materials and how effectively they present material in class. Their skill in assessing their students' progress also depends on how deeply they understand learning, and how well they can interpret students' discussions and written work. No other intervention can make the difference that a knowledgeable, skillful teacher can make in the learning process. At the same time, nothing can fully compensate for weak teaching that, despite good intentions, can result from a teacher's lack of opportunity to acquire the knowledge and skill needed to help students master the curriculum. (p. 8)

There are very few professions other than teaching in which every member has at least four years of college (and if you were to scan the personnel files of each teacher in the school, you would probably discover that a large number of teachers have masters' degrees and beyond). Teachers come to the profession with professional credentials, life experience, and sometimes experience from prior careers.

Teachers are continually learning from the environment in which they work, the staff development they participate in every year, the graduate school courses they take, and the conversations they have with their colleagues. Effective principals tap into the expertise of their teachers; they encourage teachers to share their expertise with one another; and they continually work to find ways in which teachers can further develop their expertise.

Principals who embrace teacher leadership work with teachers to identify ways to share their expertise with others. Teachers share their expertise when they serve as peer coaches, mentor beginning teachers, lead study groups, and other school-led initiatives to help fellow teachers finely hone their instructional skills. Where leadership is shared, learning and leading becomes a generative process (Zepeda, Mayers, & Benson, 2003).

Principals who support teacher learning and leading engage in what Lambert (1995) refers to as constructivist leadership: "the reciprocal processes that enable participants…to construct meanings that lead toward a common purpose" (p. 29). The common purpose is to build and to shape a vision for learning across all aspects and people in the school including teachers, students, administrators, parents, and the larger community in which the school is situated.

Teachers as Leaders Shape the Culture of the School

Culture is an elusive concept, although every school has one (see Chapter 2). A school culture can range from a positive to a negative one. Essentially, culture is "the way we do things around here" (Bower, 1966). Teacher leaders are critically important in shaping the school culture, and they are the ones who ignite the torch. A positive school culture is one in which teacher leadership is the norm and the principal supports and nurtures teachers to assume expanding roles as leaders. Principals who empower teachers to be leaders build strong school cultures because they

- Believe, from the beginning, that people have the potential and desire to succeed; then [principals] support them.

- Build on a person's strengths.

- Provide…feedback—encouragement, praise, and positive criticism —to help them grow.

- Build team spirit through retreats, cooperative efforts, and brainstorming sessions.

- Set high standards and praise results; teachers will be proud of their organization.

- Remove obstacles to teachers' success by providing the necessary resources.

- Encourage teachers to take risks, to step out and try something new.

- Make work exciting with a relaxed, positive attitude.

- Let people see the results of their work praised.

- Listen carefully. (Baloche, 1998, pp. 239–249)

The principal as instructional leader needs to examine the existing school culture to assess the viability of promoting teacher leadership. That is, a leader needs to have a starting point before looking for and cultivating teacher leadership.

A Starting Point for Teacher Leadership— Scanning the Environment

The following assessment can help principals determine the readiness for developing teacher leadership. Because each school is unique, the principal is encouraged to modify this assessment to fit better the unique context of the school and the characteristics of the school community. The principal is encouraged to assess the landscape of the organization by examining the information presented in Figure 3.1 and then develop a composite of teacher leadership at the site. The principal can assess leadership as a solo activity or engage others in the process. Others could include members of the administrative team and, of course, teachers.

Figure 3.1. Assessment of Teacher Leadership

Beliefs about teacher leadership	My beliefs about teacher leadership:	Teachers beliefs about teacher leadership:	Intersections between my beliefs and the beliefs of teachers:
History of teacher leadership	What opportunities have been afforded to teachers to emerge as teacher leaders?	Have there been organizational constraints to prevent teachers as emerging as teacher leaders?	What needs to be accomplished to bury a negative history of teacher leadership?
Risks	What risks currently exist for teacher leaders?	For each risk, ask, Is the risk is a positive or negative one?	What administrative support is needed for teachers to take risks?
Patterns of communication	Currently, how do teachers communicate with administrators?	How do administrators communicate with teachers?	What types of communication systems need to be developed to promote teacher leadership?
Training for teacher leadership	What types of training are in place for teachers who want to assume teacher leadership?	What types of training need to be developed?	What resources are needed to promote teacher leadership?
Teacher leaders	Who are the current teacher leaders?	What do these teacher leaders do to assert leadership?	Receptivity—are these teacher leaders respected by others?
External support for teacher leadership	How does the central office support teacher leadership?	How does the community-at-large support teacher leadership?	How do I support teacher leadership?

The perspectives of the principal and/or the administrative team about teacher leadership might sharply contrast those held by teachers and other members of the school (custodians, secretaries). The effective instructional leader scans the environment by including the perspectives of teachers in assessing the prevalence of teacher leadership in practice.

A strategy to involve teachers and staff in the assessment of teacher leadership is to complete an assessment on teacher leadership at the site (Figure 3.1). The questions in Figure 3.1 can be modified as necessary to keep the discussion moving. This assessment can be completed by devoting a faculty meeting or part of an inservice day to have teachers break out into small groups with each group brainstorming or recounting the teacher leadership present in the school. After small groups brainstorm, the next logical step is to have each small group report out the major ideas that emerged in small group to the rest of the faculty. During this large-group exchange, other teachers should be encouraged to add detail and perspective. When this activity concludes, the principal can cull a composite of teacher leadership. The next step of the process includes developing a plan to foster teacher leadership with the voices of teachers involved in the process.

With data aggregated from the perspectives of the administrative team and teachers, the principal needs to ask, "Now what?" The "Now what?" question is important to answer if the principal is interested in examining the context of the school and the ability of the system and its people to develop teacher leadership.

A thorny issue arises when teachers do not to want to emerge as leaders. Some teachers might not feel secure assuming new responsibilities for leading and expanded decision-making opportunities. The voices of teachers who wish not to emerge as teacher leaders need to be acknowledged with the principal and others, examining what factors (e.g., history of teacher leadership at the site, school culture, experiences of the faculty) are contributing to the reluctance of teachers to emerge as leaders. Another thorny issue arises with the tension a principal can feel in letting go of the positional power of the role of principal. This is a natural tension to experience, as it is often easier and more convenient for the principal to take the lead in getting work accomplished; however, with practice, principals can become proficient at letting go and find comfort and pride in the work that teacher leaders accomplish.

A composite picture of teacher leadership might include the information in Figure 3.2 about teacher leadership in your building. Consider the information; and, of course, this template could be used to profile teacher leadership in action in your building.

Figure 3.2. Profile of Teacher Leadership in Action

Instruction	Staff Development	Assessment	Formal Leadership	Other
Hawkins = Cooperative Learning Franklin = Socratic Methods	Doyle = Multiple Intelligences Arnold = Site Level Staff Development Representative	Parker = Authentic Assessment	Curran = Lead Teacher Jones = Language Arts Chair Günter = Third Grade Level Leader	Perkins = Peer Coach Schmidt = National Board Certified Bowman = Assertive Discipline

After profiling the teacher leaders and the work that they do to contribute to the overall leadership of the school, the principal will be in a better position to start involving more teachers in leadership—curricular, instructional, and decision making. The work of leaders is to promote leadership from within the file and rank of the organization, primarily teachers, as they are the ones who lead daily in the classroom.

The real work begins for the principal who wants to answer the question, "Now what?" The answer to this question needs to come from the principals' willingness to promote teacher leadership, the opportunities given to teachers to assume leadership, and the ability of the organization to support teachers as leaders. This process is complex to be sure, because each school has its own culture, context, and climate shaped in part by the characteristics of the people in the school, including administrators, teachers, students, parents, support staff, and central office personnel, and the larger community that the school serves.

Through scanning the school for teacher leadership, the principal might consider the skills that teacher leaders can share and the expertise that can be developed or enhanced through sharing this expertise. Shared and developing expertise will have a cumulative effect—school improvement. Figure 3.3 (p. 58) shows the range of skills that teacher leaders exert and develop through their work.

Teacher leaders bring expertise to the school, and teacher leaders are continually refining skills and knowledge and building on their expertise. As such, teacher leaders help to meet the needs of students, students, and principals by filling gaps. Gaps signal an opening or a break in continuity. Another view is that a gap is an opportunity for principals to fill a void or to extend the potential for teachers to extend their expertise to an area in need. To this end, a gap can be

Figure 3.3. Leadership Opportunities for Teachers

Teacher Leadership	*Range of Skills*
Instructional Lead Teacher	Curriculum development, peer coaching, staff development, decision making, risk taking
Department Chair	Curriculum development, peer coaching, mentoring, staff development, decision making, risk taking
Committee Chair	Collaboration, shared decision making, risk taking
Mentor	Peer coaching, reflection, inquiry, problem solving and problem posing, conflict resolution, risk taking
Teacher/Principal Selection Committee	Decision making, problem solving, conflict resolution, cooperation, risk taking, group processing
Peer Coach	Mentoring, cooperation, peer coaching, reflection, inquiry, problem solving and problem posing, conflict resolution, risk taking
Grade-Level Leader or Subject Area Coordinator	Curriculum development, peer coaching, mentoring, staff development, decision making, risk taking, action research (data collection, analysis)
Local School Council Member	Decision making, risk taking
School Improvement Team Member	Action research (data collection, analysis), decision making, risk taking
District-Level Committee Work	Collaboration, shared decision making, risk taking
After-school Childcare Coordinator	Collaboration, shared decision making, risk taking
Club Moderator/Sponsor	Collaboration, shared decision making, risk taking
Coach	Collaboration, shared decision making, risk taking
Liaison to the Larger School Community	Communication

Source: Zepeda, Mayers, & Benson (2003). Used with permission.

an opportunity for principals and teachers to work on furthering the cause of school improvement and increased learning opportunities for students.

Clark and Estes (2002) offer a strategy for filling in "performance gaps" and assert that performance gaps can only be filled "after an analysis of what is required to close a specific gap." (p. 42). The factors that need examination to fill a performance gap include (p. 43)

◆ people's knowledge and skills;

◆ their motivation to achieve the goal (particularly when compared with other work goals they must also achieve); and

◆ organizational barriers such as lack of necessary equipment and missing or inadequate work processes.

Knowledge, motivation, and organizational barriers need to be analyzed because all three factors will positively or negatively affect whether leadership for school improvement can be effectively be diffused throughout the schoolhouse.

Knowledge and Skills for Teacher Leaders

It is helpful to examine recent staff development, training, formal course-work, and other experiences (e.g., presenting at a conference) that teachers have had, because these experiences and activities help to build expertise and leadership. Principals can support the building of knowledge and skills by providing opportunities for ongoing professional growth:

◆ Sponsor membership in professional local and national organizations so teachers can take advantage of publications, conferences, and networking with other professionals who share interest and expertise.

◆ Provide opportunities for teacher leaders to attend conferences.

◆ Share professional readings from journals.

◆ Encourage teachers to return to college for advanced degrees or to work on advanced certificates (e.g., leadership).

◆ Promote teachers and their expertise throughout the district so that they can provide staff development and other learning opportunities for a wider group of teachers.

◆ Enlist teachers to serve as mentors and peer coaches within the building.

If a school system were trying to implement a new form of student assessment, the principal would need to determine the knowledge that the faculty had relative to their familiarity with the new form of assessment (e.g., performance rubrics for performance assessments). The principal would need to lead teachers into discovering what they know and what they want and need to know. Then the principal would need to tap into the resources within the building and district to help teachers extend their current knowledge or learn new skills to implement the form of assessment.

By having an understanding of these factors, principals are in a better position to assess gaps in knowledge and then develop ways to enlist teachers and others within the school to fill in these gaps. Through filling the gaps with the help of teachers, principals meet two needs—the needs of the organization and the needs of teachers who want to learn and develop as leaders within the school.

To help find gaps in knowledge, the principal might try the following strategy, one borrowed from a classroom assessment practice: K-W-L—what do you KNOW, what do you WANT to know, and what have you LEARNED? (See Figure 3.4.) Returning to the assessment example, consider this activity for assessing possible performance gaps. In a small group, ask teachers to brainstorm the following topics using Figure 3.4 as a guide.

Figure 3.4. K-W-L: Filling Gaps

KNOW	What do you KNOW about authentic assessment of student work?
	♦ What data inform this knowledge?
	♦ How did you obtain these data?
	♦ What does this information mean to your present comfort level?
WANT TO KNOW	What do you WANT to learn?
	♦ Given what you know about your current skill level, what do you want to learn? (Where are the gaps?)
	♦ How do you think you want to learn?
	♦ What will be needed for you to become comfortable with learning new information?
HAVE LEARNED	What have you LEARNED?
	♦ After staff development (formal, informal), coursework, and readings from study groups, what have you learned?
	♦ How will you apply this new knowledge?
	♦ What supports do you need to continue expanding your skills and to develop expertise?

Motivation for Teacher Leaders

To fill a gap, teachers have to be motivated to move from where they are to a new place. Teachers need to expand skills, learn new skills, and take the risks associated with learning new information and applying this information in practice. Maslow's (1987) theory of human motivation clarifies the meaning and significance that people place on work. According to Maslow, human needs extend from the physiological (lowest) to self-actualization (highest). Figure 3.5 illustrates the range of human needs according to Maslow.

Figure 3.5. Maslow's Hierarchy of Needs

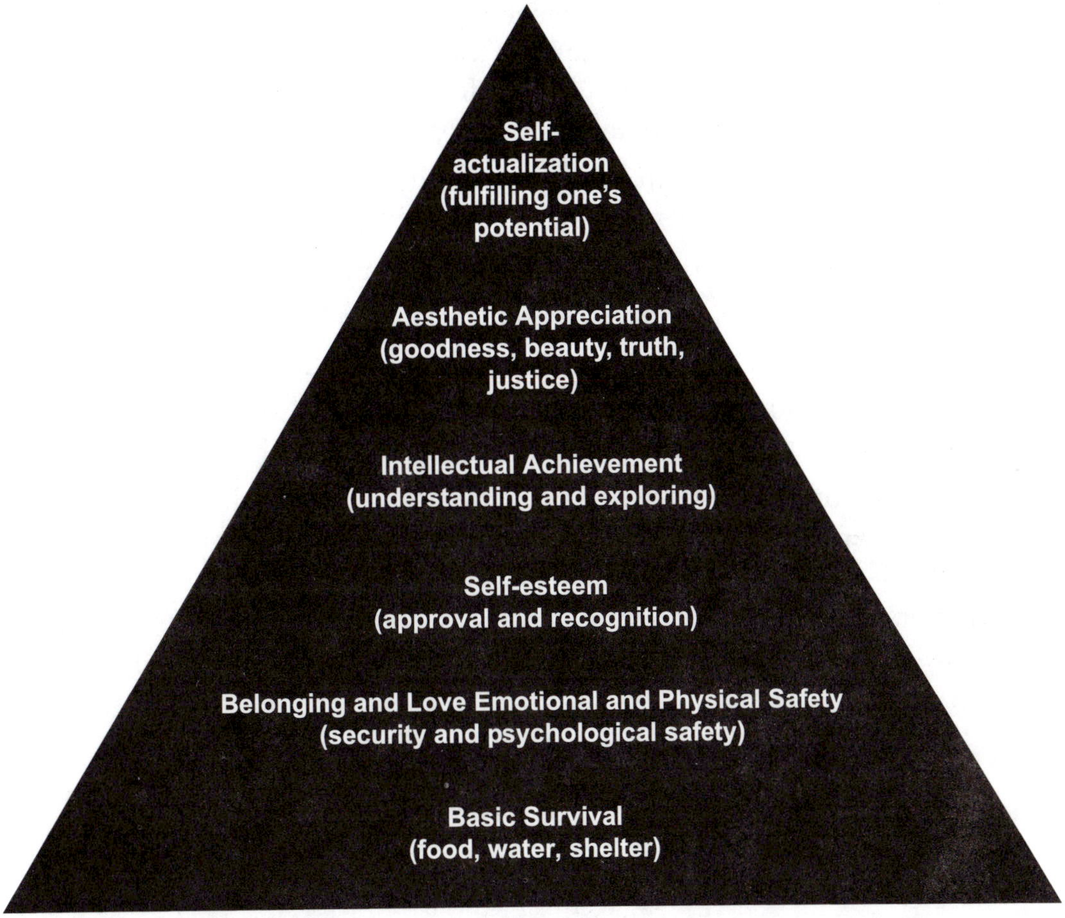

Self-actualization
(fulfilling one's potential)

Aesthetic Appreciation
(goodness, beauty, truth, justice)

Intellectual Achievement
(understanding and exploring)

Self-esteem
(approval and recognition)

Belonging and Love Emotional and Physical Safety
(security and psychological safety)

Basic Survival
(food, water, shelter)

Source: Adapted from Lefrancois (1982); Maslow (1987); Woolfolk (1990).

Teachers want to feel psychologically safe and secure and have a sense of belongingness with others. Teachers want to be productive and to feel useful. As teachers mature, they want to assume more leadership within the school, to give back what has been given to them. Motivated teachers are empowered to develop and grow while making a difference in the lives of others. Empowerment is a motivator especially for teachers who in the mid- to late-career stages seek recognition for their expertise and their positive contributions over the years.

Organizational Barriers to the Emergence of Teacher Leadership

Principals are in a prime position to help remove barriers to teachers as they try to fill in the gaps or while they are exerting teacher leadership to help others acquire new skills and knowledge. Principals remove organizational barriers by

- Removing time pressures for learning or closing performance gaps.

- Providing opportunities for teachers to interact with one another in new ways—providing release time for teachers to both observe one another teach and then provide time for teachers to reconstruct what they observed in classrooms.

- Promoting horizontal and vertical communication across grade levels, within grade levels, and across and within subject areas.

- Circulating information freely across all members of the school.

- Allocating resources to areas in need of improvement.

- Building bridges through the development of relationships within the organization—in the school, in the district, and within the broader community that the school serves.

Effective instructional leaders reconfigure their role to design continuous learning for everyone in the school organization, and they strive to provide the conditions necessary for teachers to lead (Fullan, 1997).

Another way to scan the environment to see how teacher leadership can be used to achieve school goals is to identify

- What work is in progress by teacher leaders?

- What work could be undertaken by teacher leaders?

- What is the time frame in which this work should begin?

- What teachers have interest, expertise, and time to engage in this work?

- What support is needed by teachers to assume new work and responsibilities?

There will be other questions that will need to be asked and answered as principals work at empowering teachers to assume more leadership, and these questions should be used as a guide in the development of other questions. The real work for principals to support the emergence of teacher leadership is to cultivate the talent of teachers.

Cultivating Teacher Leadership

Given opportunity, support, and affirmation, most teachers will respond to the call to leadership (Zepeda, Mayers, & Benson, 2003); they desire to emerge as leaders beyond the confines of the classrooms. Effective principals

- Create opportunities for more teachers to share their expertise.

- Develop an ethos of support and care to nurture teacher leadership through mentoring teachers through the process of evolving as leaders.

- Embed leadership as learning opportunities in the day-to-day work of teachers.

How do principals accomplish this? They accomplish this by providing professional development and mentoring for teacher leaders while encouraging risk taking.

Provide Professional Development and Mentoring for Teacher Leaders

Teachers come to the profession with varying experiences and backgrounds, and they develop skills needed to organize instruction, assess learning, manage a room full of children, and communicate with children and parents. However, when teacher leaders assume leadership, they are called on to exert different skills that go beyond the day-to-day work of the classroom. For example, teachers interact with students daily; however, teacher leaders extend communication beyond the classroom, and they might need assistance learning how to communicate differently, that is, with other adults. Closely related to communication are group-processing skills such as reaching consensus and conflict resolution; using these skills with adults is much different than with children.

Principals recognize these needs, and they provide opportunities for teacher leaders to participate in professional development aimed at enhancing leadership and the myriad skills that make good leaders better leaders. Professional development can include, for example, opportunities to

- Shadow other teacher leaders over sustained time.

- Attend professional meetings, conferences, and workshops.

- Enroll in graduate school coursework in leadership.

- Get on a list-serve of teacher leaders and engage in the talk of leadership with peers.

♦ Read professional journals, participate in professional reading and discussion groups, or join a group interested in solving a schoolwide problem. (Zepeda, Mayers, & Benson, 2003)

Teacher leaders need opportunities for learning how to further leadership skills, and mentoring and induction to the culture of leadership is a prerequisite to supporting new teacher leaders. Like beginning teachers, teacher leaders new to a position or role need assistance as they learn the work of teacher leadership, and effective principals provide the support necessary for teachers to take the risks associated with leadership.

Assuming Leadership Can Be Risky Business for the Newcomer to Leadership

Teachers who are risk takers, according to Stone (1995), "experience the freedom to take risks, which is important for growth and change," and furthermore, "Empowerment enlightens the teacher to the positive side of failure—learning what does not work and then trying again to find out what does" (p. 295). For teacher leaders to take risks, they need the support and encouragement from the principal. Teacher leaders can experience the positive side of failure and the growth and development from insights gained through taking the risk needed to succeed.

New leaders need time to learn the work of teacher leadership, and they need guidance and support as they exert leadership. Time is well spent engaging the new teacher leader in the "talk of leadership," leading the newcomer to make sense of her work. Making sense of experience includes not only talk (over extended time) but also multiple opportunities to reflect on the meanings of work. Dialogue, reflection, and a return to experience will assist the new teacher leader to make significant contributions to her work as a leader.

Suggested Readings

Katzenbach, J. R., & Smith, D. K. (1993). *The wisdom of teams: Creating the high performance organization.* Boston: Harvard Business School Press.

Katzenmeyer, M., & Moller, G. (1996). *Awakening the sleeping giant: Leadership development for teachers.* Newbury Park, CA: Corwin Press.

Lieberman, A., & Miller, L. (1999). *Teachers—transforming their world and their work.* New York: Teachers College Press.

Short, R., & Greer, J. (1997). *Leadership for empowered schools.* Columbus, OH: Merrill.

Zepeda, S. J., Mayers, R. S., & Benson, B. N. (2003). *The call to teacher leadership.* Larchmont, NY: Eye on Education.

4

Principals Build Strong Teams to Sustain School Improvement

In this Chapter…

♦ The work of creating school improvement teams

♦ Up-front work needed to develop teams

♦ Ongoing work needed to maintain the work of teams

♦ Support structures for teamwork

Introducing School Improvement Teams

School improvement efforts, no matter how small or large, can be more effectively approached through the work of teams. *Effective* teams can accomplish more than what is possible through individual efforts because teams unify people and purpose. Many people use the words *teams*, *groups*, and *committees* interchangeably. For the purposes of this book, the word *team* is used, and this designation is important in light of the discussion on teacher leadership (see Chapter 3).

Principals who support teacher leadership opportunities do more than work with groups, they cultivate the capacity for leadership among many teachers, who in turn, promote leadership among more teachers. Just about every school has a school improvement team that works on framing the work needed to achieve improvement. Some schools have several subgroups that work alongside the school improvement team. Regardless of the configuration of the school improvement process and the work that must be accomplished, there will more than likely be several teams of teachers working together, and this is why team development is so very critical.

The next logical step in promoting leadership that is iterative (Lieberman & Miller, 1999) is to work at developing teams of teacher leaders who can lead others toward school improvement. Team structures are ideally suited to promote teacher leadership because in effective teams

- ♦ Leadership is rotated among members.

- ♦ Team members are interdependent—they are accountable to each other on an equal playing field.

- ♦ Decisions are made collaboratively among team members, and this increases the commitment to the work of the team.

- ♦ The team upholds a purpose, a set of goals, and a vision for the work of the team.

- ♦ The team structure promotes participative meetings and collective work that is shared equally and equitably among team members.

If nurtured, people working together for the common good can yield many positive results. Positive results can include reduced isolation, the generation and refinement of ideas and approaches, and synergy from working with others, who, if the conditions are right, may agree and disagree with one another. The reader is encouraged to examine the Case Study in Chapter 5, in which teams were nurtured to work collaboratively on school improvement. Although the team structure at Lindsey Elementary School has taken four years to implement, the willingness of the principal and teachers to adjust the team structures has yielded many benefits for teachers, students, and parents.

Teams, regardless of their composition or the work they strive to achieve, are either *effective* or *ineffective*. Without teams, school improvement will not likely occur, and this is why the development of effective teams of teacher leaders is important for principals. Wheatley (n.d.) offers several pervasive reasons for leaders to affirm the possibilities of teams, and leaders who encourage teachers to work beyond their own, individual causes are *life affirming leaders* who

- ♦ Know they cannot lead alone. No one person is smart enough to know what to do.

- ♦ Have more faith in people than they do in themselves, and patiently and courageously insist on their participation.

- ♦ Recognize human diversity as a gift, and the human spirit as a blessing.

- ♦ Know that people only support what they create and only will act responsibly for things they care about.

- ♦ Solve unsolvable problems by bringing new voices into the room.

- ♦ Continually expand who is included in decision making.

- ♦ Convene and host conversations that really matter.

♦ Know that trust and caring make everything possible.

♦ Offer meaningful work as the greatest motivator.

♦ Freely express gratitude, appreciation, and love.

Source: http://www.fromthefourdirections.org/tpl/ourarticles.tpl

The Work of Creating School Improvement Teams

Recently, I worked with an administrative team interested in building stronger teams of teachers within their school. The school population consists of 2,800 students, 200 teachers and classified staff, and 9 full-time administrators. During the first session, the administrative team was split into three groups, and they brainstormed about what they believed to be the characteristics of effective and ineffective teams. When the small groups reconvened as a larger whole, they shared their ideas with each other. The second phase included clustering ideas (e.g., goals) and then further delineating the positive or negative attributes of each. Through this process, the administrative team charted their beliefs about what makes for either an effective or ineffective team.

Later, the administrative team used this same strategy to get teachers thinking about teams as a way to extend leadership throughout the school. Eventually, the faculty agreed on their own set of characteristics of effective teams, and they made the commitment, with the support of the administration, to develop *multiple* school improvement teams. To this day, teams work through the issues affecting the school, and teachers enjoy a new status—they are leaders working alongside the administration at finding ways to improve the instructional program.

Characteristics of Effective Teams

From the work of the teachers and administrators in this school emerged a composite of what makes for effective teams (Figure 4.1, p. 68).

Figure 4.1. Characteristics of Effective and Ineffective Teams

Effective Teams	*Ineffective Teams*
Clear Goals:	**Ambiguous Goals:**
♦ Focus and organize work, tasks, and meetings.	♦ Create unfocused, unstructured, and counter-productive work.
♦ Share vision/mission.	♦ Chaotic— lack direction.
Diffused Power:	**Limiting Power:**
♦ Have power to act and implement decisions.	♦ Have power struggles and unequal distribution of power, creating unhealthy conflict.
	♦ Are power seekers.
Balanced Membership:	**Imbalanced Membership:**
♦ Have diversity of membership; inclusion is based on expertise, and membership is decided democratically.	♦ Have forced participation; the elite participate.
Positive Behavior of Members:	**Negative Behavior of Members:**
♦ Team spirit and collaborative	♦ Personal agendas
♦ Value for team members	♦ Cynicism "I" instead of "us"
♦ Mutual respect and trust	♦ Lack of respect among members
♦ Open-minded, efficient, and flexible	♦ Dictatorial behaviors
	♦ Close-minded
Positive Conflict:	**Negative Conflict**
♦ Confidant sharing opinions	♦ Conflict of interest among members
♦ Can reach consensus	♦ Personal attacks, back-biting
♦ Problem solvers	
♦ Conflict resolution skills	
Positive Work Patterns	**Negative Work Patterns**
♦ Work is evenly distributed and distributed based on interest and expertise.	♦ Members are overburdened by details and tasks.
♦ Members are motivated to learn together.	♦ Members are overextended.
	♦ Members are not motivated to work on tasks.
	♦ Division exists among members.
Positive Support	**Lack of Support**
♦ Members can find resources, are given authority to make decisions, and know about decision-making authority from the start.	♦ Teams lack time and resources to do the job.
	♦ Authority is ambiguous.
Positive Communication	**Destructive Communication**
♦ Open communication	♦ Fearful of disagreement
♦ Constructive feedback on work and progress	♦ Poor communication and listening skills
♦ Positive communication (within the group and with external audiences)	♦ Dishonesty among members
	♦ Adversarial
Open Risk Taking	**Closed Risk Taking**
♦ Teams are motivated to accomplish goals.	♦ Members are afraid to take risks—because of possible retribution.
♦ Risk taking is encouraged.	♦ Apathy exists among group members.
	♦ Teams lack ownership of goals.

What's Next?

The ideas generated by this administrative team can serve as a model for framing the development of teams; however, building effective teams does not magically unfold because there is the desire to form them. Building effective teams is a complex, multifaceted process that takes (1) up-front work and (2) ongoing work (maintenance). The up-front work includes

   ♦ Establishing purposes and a vision for the end results

   ♦ Setting goals

   ♦ Selection of team members

Up-Front Work
Needed to Develop Teams

Establishing Purposes and a
Vision for the End Results

Teams need a purpose—there has to be a reason for forming a team—and the purpose needs to have meaning for team members (Katzenbach & Smith, 1993). Without a purpose, team members waste valuable time. One strategy is for the principal to etch out what in the end needs to be accomplished by the team (Calabrese & Zepeda, 1997). For example, if there is a need to examine why students in your school score lower in language arts on standardized tests than students in other schools in the district, the first step is to define the purpose of why the team is being formed and what the end result should be.

> *Purpose:* To examine broadly why fifth-grade students are not faring well on standardized tests.
>
> *End Result:* To develop strategies to assist students learn language arts skills for the test and beyond.

Framing the purpose from the perspective only of the principal is not enough; the members of the team need a voice in determining the purpose. Effective leaders bring the issues to the team and enlist their input on what the purpose and end result should be. This makes sense if you believe that those closest to the situation—the teachers who instruct students—will be able to create a purpose that most immediately fits the need of the school. By including team members in the development of the purpose and the end result needed to address the issues, there will be more buy-in to the overall work that the team will do. The principal could use a form similar to the one below to help team members develop the purposes and ends of the work to be accomplished.

Purpose:
End Result:

Because the purpose serves as the compass for the work of the team, the purpose needs to be established early; however, it is likely that the purpose of the team may shift as team members tackle their work.

Setting Goals

Closely related to the purpose are the goals of the team. Successful teams have "goals and values [that] are clear; they are understood and accepted by everyone [because] people are oriented to goals and results" (Dyer, 1995, p. 15). The work of the principal is to have a purpose and an end in mind, but it is more important for the principal to be open to the input of the team. From the collective points of view shared by team members, the evolving nature of group development stages that the team members will experience as they begin to work with one another, and the evolving nature of what is discovered through the work of the team, the goals might need to shift to reflect what is learned throughout these processes. However, just like the purpose, goals must be clear; team members must understand them; and goals must be linked to the team's purpose. The Goal Checklist serves as a primer on the development of goals.

Goal Checklist—Attributes of Goals

Lunenburg (1995) suggests that goals should be

♦ **Specific:** Goals are *specific* when they are clearly stated.

♦ **Measurable:** *Measurable* goals are precise and can be measured over time.

♦ **Achievable:** Goals are *achievable* if they are realistic. The effort needed to reach a goal can inspire greater effort; unrealistic goals are self-defeating.

♦ **Relevant:** Goals are *relevant* if they are viewed as important to the individual and to the team. Superficial goals are forgotten because they lack meaning.

♦ **Trackable:** Goals need to be *trackable* to check progress. Goals should not be so numerous or complex that they confuse rather than direct teams.

♦ **Ongoing:** Not all goals will be completed by the end of a specified period. Some goals are achieved over a longer time; others can be reached more quickly.

Once the purpose and ends are agreed on, the team begins the process of formulating goals as a means to prioritize work (often one at a time or many simultaneously, because the work of teams is often interlocking—one goal is related to the next). One approach is to ask the team, "What do you want to accomplish?" The next step is to track responses and then have team members prioritize the goals, keeping in mind the purpose of the team's work and the desired end results.

What do you want to accomplish?	Responses	Prioritized	End Result

Through the process of developing team goals, every member is aware of "what" they are working toward as a group. Team development, like goal development, is an iterative process with interplay among team members and the process of developing as a team. The development and agreement of goals can be tracked, expanding on the purpose(s) and end result(s). A grid to track this information can help to keep the work of the team at the forefront of all efforts.

Purpose:		
End Result:		
Goals: 1. 2. 3. 4. 5.	Resources Needed to Accomplish Goals:	Benchmarks of Achieving Goals:

Selection of Team Members

Teams comprise people who, in the end, need to be able to work with one another to achieve results. How team members interact with one another and the stages of team development are addressed in the ongoing maintenance of teams and the work that principals need to do to ensure that teams focus on the purposes, goals, and end results. Team membership can be constituted (and in some cases, reconstituted) in numerous ways. Principals can seek volunteers, ask teachers to nominate members, or handpick members.

In school systems where teams are the norm, constituting a team is part of the work-life of the school. The work of teams is viewed as a professional development opportunity and an opportunity to diffuse leadership—decision making and charting the course of the school. In schools where teamwork is new, the principal will need to take time and expend energy to cultivate the value of teamwork to achieving improvement by examining the culture of the school and the history of teams in the school. (See Chapter 2 for a discussion of building collaborative cultures and the implications for teams.)

**The History of Teams—
Knowing the Past Informs the Present**

Leaders, when selecting team members, know the history of teamwork within the context of the school. Leaders find out

♦ What is the history of teams at the site?

♦ What teams are currently in place? How long have these teams been in place?

♦ What artifacts do teams have? (Meeting summaries, action plans)

♦ How are members selected?

♦ How many people in the building are currently members of a team? Does membership on teams overlap?

♦ Who leads the teams?

♦ How many teams are active (meet regularly) or inactive (rarely meet)?

When forming teams, the principal needs to consider many variables, including

♦ The work of the team: goals, objectives, tasks, and projects that occupy the team's efforts.

♦ The types of expertise and experience needed to accomplish the team's work.

♦ Interest level: members of the faculty who have an emotional interest in the work of the team.

♦ Special interest groups: clusters of people who are committed to this work. (Calabrese & Zepeda, 1997, pp. 183–184)

Effective principals are empowering, and they encourage teachers to lead. They promote the development of teams that can work without the formal leadership of the principal having to be present; however, they realize that there is ongoing (maintenance) work that needs consideration for teams to accomplish purposes, goals, and end results.

Ongoing Work Needed to Maintain the Work of Teams

For teams to flourish, they need ongoing team maintenance that includes leadership from the principal on the sidelines. Principals assist teams by

♦ Leading teams through group development stages

♦ Providing support structures for teamwork

♦ Handling conflicts

Leading Teams Through Group Development Stages

There are five common stages that groups go through, and effective principals understand the stages and lead, or encourage others to lead, accordingly. The commonly accepted stages of group development, according to Tuckman (1965), are

♦ Stage 1. *Forming:* Members are scanning the team looking for sources of leadership; controversy is avoided; members look for safety and engage in guarded conversations. The forming stage is the orientation to the work, tasks, and goals of the team. Initial concerns emerge. To get to the next stage, storming, team members begin to take risks and offer differing points of view that lead to storming.

♦ Stage 2. *Storming:* The storming stage is marked by testing the waters and conflict. Without storming, agreeing to disagree with one another, the team members will not move toward interdependence (see norming stage).

Some principals try to bypass the storming stage by choosing people who like each other, who do not rock the boat, or who are complacent enough about issues to get to a quick-fix solution. Team members chosen with these criteria will achieve little to help the school move toward improvement and development.

Conflict occurs because members are preoccupied with proving themselves and their roles relative to expertise, leadership, and position within the team. Members move from an individual orientation to a team orientation to organize for teamwork. This move involves conflict. Conflict arises over positioning who is going to do what, deadlines, authority to make decisions, and possible power struggles among members of the team. Members learn that they have to make concessions about their own beliefs to achieve the work of the team. Interdependence between team members will not occur until the team has unearthed distrust and conflict. Conflict subsides, and the team is ready to transition to the next stage, norming.

♦ Stage 3. *Norming:* Team members adapt a common working method, and everyone is usually willing to share in this. During this phase, team members are able to reconcile their own opinions with the greater needs of the team. Cooperation and collaboration replace the conflict and mistrust of the previous phase. (The Teal Trust, www.teal.org.uk © 2002, Used with permission.) Teams having gone through the storming and norming stages can begin performing.

♦ Stage 4. *Performing:* The emphasis is now on reaching the team goals rather than working on team process. Relationships are settled, and team members are likely to build loyalty toward each other. The team is able to manage more complex tasks and cope with greater change. (The Teal Trust, www.teal.org.uk © 2002, Used with permission.)

♦ Stage 5. *Adjourning:* The work of the team is complete, and the end result has been reached. For some team members, adjourning includes feeling a sense of loss for the work of the team and bonds of interdependence formed through the team development process and completion of meaningful work.

Every team has a leader, whether it is the principal or a leader chosen from within the team such as a teacher, school counselor, social worker, school secretary. Perhaps the most important stages for the principal are the forming, storming, norming, and performing stages. It is during these stages that the group dynamics, interactions, and performances (meeting goals) of the team as a whole emerges, and it is during these stages that the work of the team will be effective in meeting the ends or ineffective by derailing from the work of the team.

Figure 4.2 shows the role of leadership across stages of group development (e.g., forming, norming, storming) by examining area in each one of these stages such as team members' reactions to leadership, the team process, trust (in the process and with team members), and how decisions are made. All of these aspects could have either positive or negative impact on the work of the team and the relationships between team members and the principal. Although variations will exist, the principal could use this information as a guide to understand the leadership needed during each stage.

Figure 4.2. The Team Process and Leadership Considerations

	Forming	*Storming*	*Norming*	*Performing*
Team Leader's Style	Leader takes a more directive approach, outlining how the process will develop and laying down a clear structure.	Leader needs to be supportive, actively listening to team members, managing conflicts, generating ideas, and explaining decisions.	Leader acts as a team member, as leadership is starting to be shared. Leader helps to develop consensus.	Leader takes overview, but within the day-to-day running, the group shares leadership between members.
Reaction to Leadership	Team members take a tentative, wait-and-see approach. Leader will be allowed to lead, but that doesn't guarantee support.	Leader is under pressure from more vociferous team members.	General support exists for the leadership within the team. Mutual respect underpins this.	Personal relationships have developed that underpin the leadership relationship.
Team Process	Process is driven by the leader. Some people are reluctant to contribute openly.	Process likely to break down until conflict is resolved.	The core process should operate smoothly, although there is a danger of focusing on smaller process issues rather than core teamwork.	Process functions well and is adjusted as necessary. Leadership is shared and tasks delegated.
Trust within the Team	Individuals are not clear about their contribution. "Getting to know you" phase. Trust may start to be built.	Trust is focused into smaller groups as subgroups and alliances form.	As roles are accepted and clarified, trust and relationships start to develop to a greater degree.	Team starts to operate on higher levels of trust as loyalty and relationships develop.
How Decisions are Made	Nominated leader is expected to make decisions. Some more vocal members may dominate.	Decisions are hard to make. Members are unwilling to give way. Compromise is a frequent outcome.	Group is able to come to common decisions. Win-win is more likely than compromise.	Decision making is easier—some decisions are delegated to subgroups or individuals.

Source: *The Team Process.* Copyright by The Teal Trust (www.teal.org.uk) © 2002. Used with permission. http://www.teal.org.uk/et/teampro.htm

Providing Support
Structures for Teamwork

To thrive, teams need a supportive structure, and this is where the leadership of the principal is needed. Teams need

♦ *Opportunities to meet*: Time during the day needs to be provided. Team members will be resistant to serving on teams if the only time available is on their own time—before and after school or during personal plan or lunchtime.

♦ *Resources*: Resources include, for example, secretarial support to assist with preparing materials (photocopying) and distributing materials to nonteam members. Teams cannot make good decisions unless they have data (e.g., test scores, discipline records, curriculum and teaching guides), and often accessing data in a school system is an elusive process for teachers. Principals can facilitate the work of teams by gathering data and helping teams understand what the data mean.

♦ *Training:* Because of the inherent structures of working in isolation, many teachers who have the desire to work with others may not have the skills needed to work in teams. The National School Boards Foundation, in conjunction with the National School Board Association, believes well-functioning teams have 10 basic characteristics (Figure 4.3) that enable them to achieve purposes and ends.

♦ *Communication and monitoring:* Team members do not want to feel that they have been delegated to do the work of the administration. Principals need to monitor the work of teams, provide information, and help teams communicate with the larger community.

♦ *Commitment from the top:* Teams need a firm commitment from the principal that the work of the team will be supported from the beginning to the end of the process.

♦ *Leadership from the sidelines:* Principals will need to take on a new role—leading from the sidelines—in other words, getting out of the way so that the team can develop and work through conflict, work, solutions, and so forth.

♦ *Skill development in critical areas for team leaders:* Teams comprise teachers and other school personnel who may be leaders but who are, for the first time, serving as the leader of the team. Critical areas can range from conflict resolution to running an effective meeting. All teams meet, and to this end, the meeting itself will set the tone for the work of the team. People do not like to attend meetings where lit-

Figure 4.3. Ten Characteristics of Well-functioning Teams

Characteristics	Description
Purpose	Members proudly share a sense of why the team exists and are invested in accomplishing its mission and goals.
Priorities	Members know what needs to be done next, by whom, and by when to achieve team goals.
Roles	Members know their roles in getting tasks done and when to allow a more skillful member to do a certain task.
Decisions	Authority and decision-making lines are clearly understood.
Conflict	Conflict is dealt with openly and is considered important to decision making and personal growth.
Personal Traits	Members feel their unique personalities are appreciated and well utilized.
Norms	Group norms for working together are set and seen as standards for everyone in the groups.
Effectiveness	Members find team meetings efficient and productive and look forward to this time together.
Success	Members know clearly when the team has met with success and share in this equally and proudly.
Training	Opportunities for feedback and updating skills are provided and taken advantage of by team members.

Source: The National School Boards Foundation (n.d.). http://www.nsba.org/sbot/toolkit/LeadTeams.html.

tle is accomplished because the structure of the meeting is disorganized. This is a time waster for everyone. Figure 4.4 (pp. 78–79) presents a model to help organize team meetings that produce results.

Figure 4.4. Meeting Checklist for
Optimum Closure and Commitment

To achieve optimum closure, consensus, and commitment on any number of issues, use the following check list to prepare for a meeting.

1. When calling a meeting, decide

    ♦ What's the purpose?

    ♦ What will a successful outcome look like?

    ♦ Who must attend to reach the outcome?

2. Always circulate a clear agenda to help people prepare. It should include

    ♦ A brief description of each item and time allotted.

    ♦ What the close on each item will be (open discussion, report, decision, follow-up.

    ♦ Any special preparation needed.

3. Clear meeting roles help produce an optimal outcome. Each meeting should have

    ♦ A facilitator.

    ♦ A scribe.

    ♦ A timer.

    ♦ A closer.

4. Meetings are tools to solve business problems. The key steps in reaching closure with consensus and commitment are

    ♦ Identify the problem/issue.

    ♦ Create a recognizable goal.

    ♦ Elicit all ideas and innovations.

    ♦ Devise strategic plans for resolution.

    ♦ Create timelines and accountabilities.

    ♦ Handle slippage proactively.

    ♦ Acknowledge closure and celebrate your success.

5. A meeting write-up should be a short document of accomplishment. Try to include

    ♦ A summary of progress made on each item.

    ♦ Any team decisions made.

- ◆ Any accountabilities drawn and their timelines.

- ◆ Any other carry-forward items for your next meeting.

- ◆ Agenda, time, and place for your next meeting if possible.

6. A meeting audit can help improve the meeting process. This sheet can become a checklist for the meeting audit. Substantively, you will build a positive meeting climate if

- ◆ Everyone feels included and invited to participate.

- ◆ Communication is solution-oriented.

- ◆ Pretended commitments are avoided.

- ◆ Each item is closed in some form.

- ◆ People generously acknowledge each other's contribution.

Source: Learning Center (n.d.). *Meeting Check List from High Performance Teamwork and Quality Training Courses.* Used with permission. http://www.learningcenter.net/library/meeting.shtml.

Assessing Teams and Their Work

Teams and the work they can accomplish should not be taken for granted in the school improvement process. The principal can help teams (school improvement, grade-level, administrative) to assess what they do and the process of working in teams. Bruce Hammonds and Wayne Morris of leading-learning.co.nz provide a measure to help leaders assess teams and the work that they do, and this measure is presented as a means to assist principals in examining the work of teams (Figure 4.5, p. 80).

Figure 4.5. School as a Community:
How Good is Your Teamwork?

On a 1 to 10 scale, 10 being excellent, how does your team rate?

Does your team or school

1. Have a shared sense of purpose and a common understanding of what is required?

     0 <————————————————————> 10

2. Have open, honest communication?

     0 <————————————————————> 10

3. Have mutual respect, trust, and understanding?

     0 <————————————————————> 10

4. Handle conflict in a constructive way?

     0 <————————————————————> 10

5. Have a diverse range of skills that people take advantage of?

     0 <————————————————————> 10

6. Have effective ways of working, with access to all information, and keep records of what has been agreed to?

     0 <————————————————————> 10

7. Have teachers who act as coaches empowering others?

     0 <————————————————————> 10

8. Have time to constantly reflect, gather data and feedback to improve processes of delivering curriculum, ensuring students progress and ways of working?

     0 <————————————————————> 10

9. Help individual members recognize their needs for professional development to achieve school goals?

     0 <————————————————————> 10

10. Link with other school teams, share ideas, exchange ways of working, including visits to other schools?

     0 <————————————————————> 10

11. Have a sense of fun and comradeship?

     0 <————————————————————> 10

12. Celebrate both success and failure (good attempts) and provide support to members?

     0 <————————————————————> 10

Source: *School as a Community: How good is your teamwork?* Copyright by Bruce Hammonds and Wayne Morris of leading-learning.co.nz. Used with permission. http://www.leading-learning.co.nz/school-vision/teamwork-survey.html.

Results of such an assessment can be used to identify areas in which teams need professional development and areas in which principals need to provide assistance and intervention such as possibly reconfiguring the structure of the team to promote effectiveness. Wheelan, Tilin, and Sanford (1996) offer several tips for improving group effectiveness that can assist teams and their work.

Tips for Improving Group Effectiveness

1. *Learn about groups and how they operate.* Group effectiveness is an excellent topic for an inservice session.

2. *Discuss group functioning each time the group meets.* A brief discussion about how the group is functioning should be on the agenda of every meeting.

3. *Ask the group for feedback.* Periodically, ask group members for anonymous written feedback about group functioning and how it can be improved.

4. *Take group members' feedback seriously.* Devote a portion of the next meeting to planning ways to improve the group.

5. *Keep the focus on the group.* The biggest mistake that groups make is to place the blame for group problems on the leader, one member, or a subset of members. If group issues become personal issues, it is difficult to resolve them without the help of a consultant. When individuals feel attacked, counterattacks and cycles of revenge and retribution typically follow.

6. *Keep groups small.* Research suggests that groups of less than 10 are more cohesive, organized, and productive. If a large group cannot be reduced in size, design meetings to include time for subgroup discussions. For example, if there are 20 people at a meeting, create five groups of four members each. These subgroups discuss an issue for 20 minutes and report the highlights of their discussion to the entire group. Using this format ensures that everyone contributes to the discussion.

7. *Spend time planning how goals and tasks will be accomplished.* Don't jump too quickly into working on goals and tasks. Groups that spend time planning how they will work together are more productive in the end.

8. *Allow the group enough time to accomplish its goals and tasks.* The time frame should take into consideration the fact that groups need time to develop and coalesce. It takes about six months for groups to mature.

9. *Do not assume that implementing these suggestions is the responsibility of the group's leader.* Group effectiveness is a joint responsibility: Every member plays a role in the group's success or failure.

10. *If these suggestions don't improve things, get the help of a good consultant.* Remember, stuck groups are not bad groups, and they don't contain bad or incompetent people. If you get stuck in a doorway, sometimes it takes a push from someone else to get unstuck. The same is true for groups.

http://www.coled.umn.edu/CAREI/Reports/Rpractice/Spring96/group.htm

For the school principal who supports team structures, essentially, leadership is multiplied, and so too is the structure of the school readied for the work of planning for and achieving school improvement.

Suggested Readings

Katzenbach, J. R., & Smith, D. K. (1993). *The wisdom of teams: Creating the high performance organization.* Boston: Harvard Business School Press.

Maeroff, G. I. (1993). *Team building for school change: Equipping teachers for new roles.* New York: Teachers College Press.

Waterman, R. H., Jr. (1987). *The renewal factor.* New York: Bantam Books.

5

The Work of the Principal in Planning for School Improvement

In this Chapter…

- ◆ The broad base of involvement needed for planning for school improvement
- ◆ Communication and school improvement
- ◆ Getting started
  - ◆ Consult the school mission
  - ◆ Assemble the school improvement planning team
  - ◆ Assess the current situation of the school and students to target gaps (collect data)
  - ◆ Analyze data
  - ◆ Develop improvement goals and objectives to narrow gaps
  - ◆ Develop strategies to meet goals and objectives
  - ◆ The action plan is the school improvement plan
- ◆ Pulling it all together—a case from the field

Introducing Planning for School Improvement

According to Mintrop and MacLellan (2002), planning is "a key ingredient to the school improvement process in effective schools" (p. 276). Planning is learning because learning evolves from examining the current reality of the school situation against needs (gaps). For the principal, it is for the process of "planning for planning" that leadership is needed.

Previous chapters have examined developing a culture conducive to school improvement, promoting teacher leadership, and building strong teams as a precursor to school improvement. This chapter examines planning for school improvement and the myriad and complex work involved with planning. Schmoker and Marzano (1999) detail that effective planning

- Is a collaborative process, engaging the community of learners to develop vision, beliefs, mission, and goals;

- Involves collecting, organizing, and analyzing data;

- Reflects expectations for student achievement;

- Involves analyzing student needs;

- Involves analyzing teacher needs; and

- Includes ongoing evaluation of efforts and modifications as appropriate to sustain continuous improvement.

No lock-step formula for planning exists. However, several planning strategies can be modified to meet the contextual needs of schools and the personnel who engage in school improvement. The principal is encouraged to ask what makes sense given the context of the school, the characteristics of the school, and the needs of the school? The answer to these questions should act as a guide in the planning for school improvement.

It is impossible to plan for school improvement until the current reality of the school is understood, and this understanding is dependent on reliable data. Once the school improvement team has assembled, received the requisite training on the school improvement process, and been given the opportunity to work as a team, planning for school improvement can begin.

Planning is time-consuming and requires sustained attention to (1) assessing the current situation of the school and its students by collecting data, (2) analyzing data and identifying gaps, and (3) developing a schoolwide school improvement plan. Within each one of these broad areas of planning, there are many processes embedded within them that, if approached with openness for change and a press for ongoing development, school improvement can be achieved.

The Broad Base of Involvement Needed for Planning for School Improvement

Effective planning for school improvement is dependent on a broad base of involvement including teachers, parents, community members, students, central office personnel—anyone who is a stakeholder in the school. The Education Quality and Accountability Office (Ontario, Canada) illustrates the school as the center of the improvement process (Figure 5.1) and the interrelated and cooperative nature in which school improvement must be approached to ensure a systematic and interrelated approach to improvement efforts. Across the system, school, and classroom levels are a series of questions that can lead the principal in the overall planning, identification, and assessment of what needs to be accomplished in planning for school improvement.

Figure 5.1. Cooperative Activities for Successful Improvement Planning

System	*School*	*Classroom*
What are the needs of our schools?	What are the needs of our students?	What are the needs of my students?
How should we focus our plan?	How should we focus our planning?	How should I focus my planning?
What are our indicators of success?	What criteria shall we use as indicators of success?	What criteria shall I use for indicators of success?
What system improvements should we make?	What improvements should we make in our school?	What improvements and modifications do I want to make to my program?
How will we measure success?	How will we measure success?	How will I measure success?
How can we involve all partners?	How can we work together?	How can I best work with colleagues?
How can we involve the community?	How can we involve parents, school councils, and the community?	How can I best work with parents to improve the performance of their children?

Source: The Education Quality and Accountability Office (2000). *Ontario Report and Guide on School Improvement Planning: 1999–2000*, p. 13. Reproduced with permission.

Through such a cooperative approach to school improvement, efforts across the system (central office, school, and classroom) will align more purposefully on the development of school improvement plans and the strategies needed to bring the plan to life. Planning and then implementing and monitoring school improvement (Chapter 6) require effective communication. Information can be communicated in a variety of ways in addition to meetings. The advent of e-mail, instant messaging, and system television channels can complement parent and faculty newsletters and bulletins.

Communication and School Improvement

The importance of communication in the school improvement process cannot be underestimated. The principal needs to communicate to a variety of stakeholders. Essentially, the stakeholders include the people who broadly comprise the system, the school, and the classroom and also include external constituents (parents, local business, and civic groups).

The principal communicates the needs of the building to the central office and the vision and direction of the system back to the school. Communication within the site level is critical to keep members of the school apprised of the work of the school improvement team. Mechanisms need to be in place for teachers to communicate with one another, with members of the school improvement team, and with the principal throughout planning, implementing, and monitoring school improvement efforts.

Because of the variety of people involved in planning for school improvement, the principal needs to develop communication strategies that enhance the sharing of information. It is up to the principal to model communication that is truthful, open, and direct, which will serve as a fertile ground to promote trust among stakeholders. During planning, gaps in performance will emerge, and one of the inherent dangers in school improvement planning is the natural tendency for people to react to weaknesses or gaps in performance by placing blame on others, especially if improvement is not forthcoming immediately after strategies have been implemented (Haydn, 2001). Fink (1999) warns, "Attempting to promote change by using shame, guilt or bullying tactics will fail in the long term" in promoting overall school improvement (p. 139).

Given the press for accountability, the public now has access to information about school systems and the schools within them, including data about performance aggregated across students by gender, race, and grade level, for example. With the click of a mouse, parents can examine state department Web sites to read about how well students are performing on statewide tests, whether their school is a "safe" one, if the school is rated failing, the education level of the teachers, and other information relative to demographics reported in individual system and school report cards. State departments of education report overall ratings of schools based on test and other data.

School improvement signals change, and it is important for the principal to promote communication that keeps constituents in the proverbial communication loop of school improvement activities. The four major purposes of communication include informing, planning, asking, and evaluating.

Communication that Informs

Communication during the planning stages (also while implementing and monitoring) of school improvement is a time-intensive task; however, the principal must be committed to keeping the internal and external community aware of information related to school improvement. Because school improvement teams often comprise numerous teachers who represent grade levels, departments, subject areas, and other school personnel such as the school nurse, counselor, social worker, and ancillary staff such as cafeteria workers, and custodians in addition to central office personnel (curriculum coordinators) and in some instances community members, it falls to the principal to establish ways of sharing information of the work of school improvement. The principal can work with teams to establish ways of sharing the work accomplished in team meetings. E-mail and instant messaging can be used to share information and to elicit feedback.

Parents and the public need to be kept informed about the school's accomplishments, activities, and the efforts at school improvement. Updates on school improvement activities, including modifications in instructional strategies and curriculum, staff development, gains in student achievement, and tips on how parents can assist in the work of school improvement, can be included in press releases for the local print and broadcast media, the school district's print and broadcast media, as well as the school's Web site. The principal and members of the school improvement team and other teacher leaders can use monthly parent-organization meeting time and time earmarked for parent-teacher meeting days to communicate with parents about school improvement. Communication that informs can help to support the overall efforts of the school in accomplishing goals because communication that informs also assists with planning, implementing, and monitoring school improvement.

Communication that Helps Plan

Every aspect of planning—from developing the school improvement team to collecting and analyzing data to reporting gaps—needs to be communicated during the school improvement process. Preparing reports for the central office or the board of education is a part of the planning process. These reports usually contain a summary of past performance, current programs, and course offerings, and a forecast of future needs. The information (data) in these reports can assist in making curricular, personnel, and budgetary decisions. Looking at past meeting agendas and summaries can help the principal to frame long-term planning and track long-term goal attainment.

While assessing the current reality of the school, the principal needs to commit observations and data to writing and then share this information with faculty. Often, the principal will enlist others in the process of scanning the environment looking for clues, seeking input, and tracking data; this information also needs to be shared with the community.

Communication that Asks

Planning requires communication that asks for data from central office personnel, teachers, and others who have information needed to help with the planning process. The principal needs to reflect on what data are needed to help teachers assess the reality of the school. Later data sources will be discussed; however, the principal can get ready for planning by finding out how to access information and from whom. One strategy is for the principal to meet with the central office personnel who are responsible for information management. Many school systems now have a central office administrator who oversees school improvement and the data needed for schools to develop plans. Given the complexity of data analysis, the principal can seek assistance from local universities and regional educational agencies.

Communication that Evaluates

All schools have a school improvement plan that chronicles the current reality of the school, and the principal takes the lead in supplying the information needed to conduct an evaluation of the school's programs and course offerings. This type of communication takes skill development in scanning because the principal has to have information based on data before that information can be communicated to stakeholders.

The specific information required in this type of communication can vary depending on the school, and ironically, the school improvement plan is typically built on this information. Generally, the information included in evaluation reports consists of courses and special programs offered, enrollment trends, demographics, grade distributions, and standardized test results.

Getting Started

In the end, a school improvement plan is written; however, the plan is more than a notebook on a shelf. School improvement plans and the efforts to get to the point of writing the plan help to focus people on actions (goals, objectives, and strategies) to improve the quality of teaching and learning.

Similar to writing the introductory paragraph to a long essay, getting started for planning school improvement is difficult. The following *planning for planning* framework is offered as one way for principals to lead in the process of planning for school improvement. However, every school seeking improvement should adapt this framework to fit the particular school context because there are no absolutes.

- Consult the school mission.
- Assemble the school improvement planning team.
- Assess the current situation of the school and students to target gaps.
- Analyze data.
- Develop improvement goals and objectives to narrow gaps.
- Develop strategies to meet goals and objectives.
- Formulate the action plan, that is, the school improvement plan.

Consult the School Mission

The mission is the purpose on which all efforts of the school focus attention. A mission and its statements serve to focus a school on the beliefs and values of the school community. The mission helps to guide the principal in focusing, developing, and coordinating the school improvement process. Fielder (2003) identifies four reasons why a mission needs to be purposefully *limited* in scope:

1. It concentrates everyone's attention, energy, and efforts on accomplishing the mission. There are no activities, although enjoyable and even important, that do not lead to the mission.

2. When the mission is clear, it is much more likely that the mission will be accomplished.

3. It focuses resources into areas where they will be the most effective.

4. A limited mission provides a means by which everyone can measure the progress toward the mission. (pp. 3–5)

The mission statement is where the proverbial rubber meets the road, and the mission helps to answer fundamental questions:

- Who are we as a collective faculty and school?
- What do we want to strive to become?
- Whom do we serve?
- What are the needs of those we serve?
- What are our strengths and weaknesses?
- Where are we headed?
- How will we know when we have arrived? (Zepeda, 2003, p. 36)

Assemble the School Improvement Team

Although the principal assumes final responsibility for school improvement, the principal alone cannot achieve school improvement without the work of many others. School improvement teams evolve based on the structure of the school. Chapter 4 details the work associated with developing effective teams. Eastwood and Tallerico (1990) report 11 factors needed to support school-improvement teams (Figure 5.2).

Figure 5.2. Factors Needed to Build Effective School Improvement Teams

1. *Skill Development*: Inservice training to develop skills in shared decision making, group processes, and the effective schools research.

2. *Adequate Time to Conduct Team Business*: Time to participate fully in team planning/decision making without feeling rushed, including time to meet deadlines.

3. *Strong Administrative Support*: Administrators facilitate team functioning rather than taking a laissez-faire approach.

4. *Establishing Purpose*: Early establishment of the reasons for taking the new team approach.

5. *Team Formation*: Determining when teams should be constituted.

6. *Communication*: The vehicle for keeping all interested parties informed of what is going on.

7. *Member Selection*: Accomplished in some democratic fashion.

8. *Sharing the Plan*: Making sure that all interested parties know and understand what will be expected.

9. *Team Tasks*: Defining the responsibilities and jobs that are required of team members.

10. *Team Procedures*: Determining how the team will conduct its business.

11. *Team Size*: Determining how many members will constitute the representative team.

Source: Eastwood & Tallerico (1990, p. 5).

Assess the Current Situation of the School and Students to Target Gaps

Planning begins with conducting a needs assessment, and according to the SILC School Improvement Planning Process,

> The planning process begins with a comprehensive school profile. The school profile should tell a great deal about what's happening in a successful building. It should also help the building leadership team identify the areas in the school that need improvement. (p. 2)

Assessing the current situation entails data collection and analysis, and both qualitative and quantitative data are the backbone in framing the focus of the school improvement plan.

Data are important in the school improvement process because data frame the decisions that are made, namely, in what direction the people of the school focus school improvement efforts. Later in this chapter, a detailed case study of the development of a school improvement plan is provided; in Chapter 6 a detailed analysis of the uses of data is offered. Data are important in both planning and monitoring school improvement efforts, and this is why the uses of data are explored in this chapter and Chapter 6. In this chapter, we focus primarily on the collection, analysis, and use of data in defining gaps; in Chapter 6, we look at analysis of data on tracking student achievement as a result of school improvement efforts. In both instances, planning and monitoring, data are important.

Bennett (2002) reports that "Principals need not be victims controlled by the environment" and "administrators can…transform themselves from victim to victor, to harness the value of data-driven decision making, to empower their learning community in the process, and together, to improve their schools" (p. 1). Gandal and McGiffert (2003) suggest that school personnel "compile data from a number of sources, including classroom assignments, quizzes, diagnostic tests, and large-scale assessments" (p. 41) to provide a comprehensive picture of the needs of the school.

Assessing the learning environment can be achieved through a variety of processes including

- ♦ Environmental scanning
- ♦ Gap analysis

Environmental Scanning

According to Choo (2001), "Environmental scanning is the acquisition and use of information about events, trends, and relationships in an organization's external environment, the knowledge of which would assist management in planning the organization's future course of action" (p. 1). Moreover, Choo indicates that environmental scanning helps organizations to understand both external and internal change. Because school improvement is a type of purposeful change, Choo's perspective is important to consider:

> Organizations scan the environment to understand the external forces of change so that they may develop effective responses which secure or improve their position in the future. They scan to avoid surprises, identify threats and opportunities, gain competitive advantage, and improve long-term and short-term planning. To the extent that an organization's ability to adapt to its outside environment is dependent on knowing and interpreting the external changes that are taking place, environmental scanning constitutes a primary mode of organizational learning. Environmental scanning includes both looking at information (viewing) and looking for information (searching). (p. 2)

Gap Analysis

In Chapter 3, the process of filling the gaps was examined related to teacher leadership and development. Through the assessment of data from multiple sources, certain patterns will emerge that point toward gaps—commonly referred to as needs.

One strategy to assist with needs assessment is gap analysis. Assessment is critical in that the results will lead to identifying needs, and according to Swist (n.d.),

> A *need* is not a want or desire. It is a gap between "what is" and "what ought to be." The needs assessment serves to identify the gaps, and… the assessment is part of a planning process focusing on identifying and solving performance problems. (¶3, emphasis in the original)

Data collection and gap analysis can work in tandem:

> The data collection and gap analysis is an important phase of integrated school improvement planning and provides the basis for the development of the action plan and the budget. This phase offers the opportunity for the plan to be based on data-driven decisions rather than perceived needs. In this phase, the school improvement team collects data, analyzes data, analyzes gaps, and sets priorities for improvement (as the basis for developing measurable goals. (Illinois State Board of Education, 1999, p. 7)

A gap analysis, according to Rouda and Kusy (1995), can help to assess actual performance against existing standards. A gap is a space or an opening, and the gap is the space between where the school is and where the school wants to be. By examining gaps, school improvement teams can plan (1) where the school needs to go—the school improvement *process*—and (2) how the school is going to get to the destination—the improvement *product*.

The gaps are areas that need attention, and each gap can serve as a point of departure for developing strategies to fill the gap by addressing and remediating the areas that need improvement. The needs assessment process, according to Corson (2000), begins by starting with the end in mind and by keeping two things at the forefront of the process:

1. The desired state should be written in a measurable form so that you know if you're getting closer.

2. The current reality should be data-driven rather than based on opinions.

Corson provides a way to traverse (Figure 5.3) the gap between the current reality and the desired state. Note that the space between the current reality and the described state is the gap.

**Figure 5.3. The Gap Between Current
Reality and Desired State**

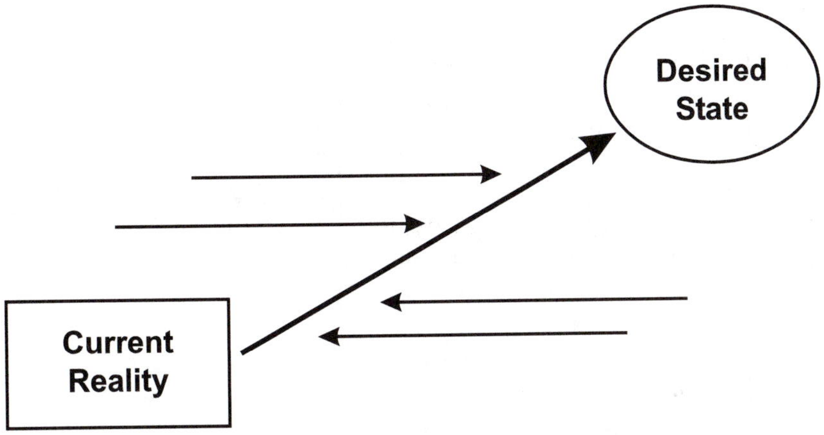

Source: Corson (2000). *Desired State Chart*. Used with permission. http://edservices. aea7.k12.ia.us/sibd/direction/desiredstate.html.

Rouda and Kusy (1995) offer sound strategies for conducting a gap analysis. Although these strategies were developed within the context of business and industry for the purposes of identifying training needs (Figure 5.4, pp. 94–95), many insights can be gleaned from the work of Rouda and Kusy and related directly to planning and assessing school improvement.

Figure 5.4. Steps to the Gap Analysis

Step	Process/Parts	Intent
Step 1: Determining the Actual (real) Performance Against New Standards	1. Identify Current Situation: Analysis should examine organizational goals, climate, and internal and external constraints. 2. Identify Desired or Necessary Situation: Work centers on identifying the desired or necessary conditions for organizational and personal success. This analysis focuses on the necessary job tasks/standards, as well as the skills, knowledge, and abilities needed to accomplish these successfully. It is important to identify the critical tasks necessary, and not just observe our current practices. We also must distinguish our actual needs from our perceived needs, our wants.	To find the gap. The gap is the difference between the current and the necessary. The gaps will help to identify needs, purposes, and objectives. By focusing on the gaps, organizations can more readily focus on 1. Problems or deficits 2. Impending change 3. Opportunities 4. Strengths 5. New directions 6. Training and development
Step 2: Identify Priorities and Importance	From the gaps identified in Step 1, examine gaps in view of their importance to organizational goals, realities, and constraints. Determine if the identified needs are real, if they are worth addressing, and specify their importance and urgency in view of organizational needs.	Prioritize what is most important and why.
Step 3: Identify Causes of Performance Problems and/or Opportunities	Identify specific problem areas and opportunities in the organization.	Prepare for the future so that solutions can be developed for the current situation and in preparation for the future. This is the time for community members to analyze what they are doing and the impact the what is having on the environment.

Step	Process/Parts	Intent
Step 4: Identify Possible Solutions and Growth Opportunities	Training and/or other interventions might be called for if sufficient importance is attached to moving our people and their performance into new directions.	Help people see and understand the importance of ongoing professional growth to fill a gap. *Training* may be the solution, *if* there is a knowledge problem. *Organization development* activities may provide solutions when the problem is not based on a lack of knowledge and is primarily associated with systematic change. These interventions might include strategic planning, organization restructuring, performance management and/or effective team building.

Source: Rouda and Kusy (1995). *Needs assessment: The first step.* Used with permission. All rights reserved. http://www.alumni.caltech.edu/~rouda/T2_NA.html

Analyze Data

Data should drive the development of the school improvement plan. Data serve two critical purposes that guide the school improvement process:

> Collection and careful analysis of pertinent information is critical in determining the effectiveness of the existing programs and services in your school. Moreover, the types of data collected for the profile can assist schools in planning and sustaining their school improvement initiatives on behalf of student learning. (Fitzpatrick, 1997, p. 13)

Securing data for the school improvement team is an area in which the principal needs to take the lead. Most school systems have the technology to report data across sources on student attendance, discipline referrals, standardized test results, free and reduced lunches, demographic profiles, and the like.

Data often can be disaggregated across schools, grade levels, subject areas, and teachers. Bernhardt (2002) identifies four types of data to guide collection and analysis:

1. *Demographic data* are needed to describe the school context. These data provide the over-arching context for everything that the school does with respect to school improvement. These contextual data show who the students, staff, and community are, and how they have changed over time.

2. *Perceptual data* can tell schools about student, parent, and staff satisfaction with the work of the school. Perceptual data can also help the school understand what is possible in the big picture of school improvement and what has been done internally to meet school improvement goals.

3. *Student learning data* help schools see the results they are getting now. These data tell schools which students are succeeding academically and which are not. They also guide planning, leadership, partnership, and professional development efforts.

4. *School process data* provide staff with information about their current approaches to teaching and learning, programs, and the learning organization. It is these processes that will need to change to achieve different results. (p. 46, Emphasis in the original)

Figure 5.5 provides possible sources for demographic, perceptual, student learning, and school process data.

Bernhardt (2002) indicates that

collectively and interactively, these data begin to inform schools of the impact of current programs and processes on their students—so they can decide what to change to get different results. These data can also assist schools in understanding the root causes of problems as opposed to just focusing on symptoms. (p. 47)

Figure 5.5. Possible Sources for Data

Data Types	*Possible Sources of Data*
Demographic data Answers the question: Who are we at our school?	◆ Enrollment and enrollment patterns ◆ Attendance patterns ◆ Number of suspensions, unexcused absences, tardies, and dropout rates disaggregated by race, gender, special education ◆ Student mobility trends ◆ Ethnic composition of students ◆ Number of students who receive free and reduced meals (breakfast and lunch) ◆ Family backgrounds (one- and two-parent households, family incomes, education levels of parents, parent occupations) ◆ Number of faculty and staff members (staff turnover rates, in-district transfers, retirements, resignations) ◆ Classified personnel ◆ Education levels of teachersExperience levels of teachers
Perceptual data Answers the question: How pleased are stakeholders with the school and its programs?	Many school systems use the services of professionals such as the National Study of School Evaluation (NSSE) as a means to gather data from parents, teachers, students, and others who have a stake in school improvement.
Student learning data Answer the questions: How well do our students achieve? Is the achievement of all students improving?	◆ National measures (e.g., Iowa Basic Skills, ACT) ◆ State measures (e.g., the Georgia Kindergarten Assessment Program [GKAP], an assessment for kindergarten students to determine readiness for first grade, and the Georgia Criterion Referenced Competency Test [CRCT], which measures students performance in reading, language arts, and math) ◆ System Measures (e.g., instruments developed by school systems to measure student learning in key areas such as math, science, social studies, and language arts)
School process data Answer the question: What are our current programs and how well do these programs serve our students?	◆ Length of the school day ◆ Description of the academic program, counseling services, and special education services ◆ Special programs (e.g., ESOL, gifted and early intervention programs, physical and occupational therapy services) ◆ Technology and its integration ◆ Cocurricular and extracurricular activities (e.g., spelling and geography bees, math bowl, clubs, student council, athletics, service learning) ◆ Parental support (PTA, PTO, parent volunteers, booster clubs)

Figure 5.6 illustrates the collective and interactive nature of data related to measuring impact.

Figure 5.6. Multiple Measures of Data

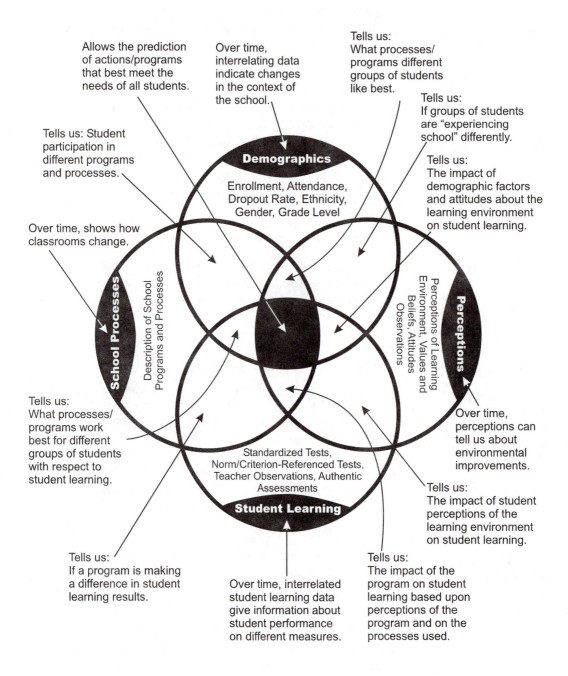

Source: Bernhardt (2002, p. 48). Reprinted with permission.

Much of these data are readily available, and Corson (2002) suggests that before collecting data, consider the data readily available, as illustrated in Figure 5.7.

Figure 5.7. Data Sources in Schools

Data You May Already Have

- norm-referenced testing data
- criterion-referenced testing data
- state assessment testing data
- grade distributions and GPA
- attendance patterns
- discipline records
- illness patterns
- guidance services referrals
- surveys—teacher, student, parent, business
- needs assessmentsportfolio assessments
- exit outcomes and exit projects

Student Data

- attendance rates
- retention rates
- suspension, expulsion, and dropout rates
- achievement and failure patterns
- standardized test scores
- issues of school climate
- any readily available entry-level characteristics of students in the school
- any follow-up information about graduates
- any other issues that the instructional staff believes to be impacting student performance in the school

Instructional Data

- curriculum (e.g., number of courses by grade) school organization
- teacher/student ratios
- most common instructional techniques used, focusing on their link to results
- summary of available learning support systems
- a definition of who is responsible for monitoring student progress and communicating this information to others
- teacher attendance rates

Community Data

- socioeconomic factors
- geographic factors
- political factors
- religious factorsracial and ethnic factors
- national/international factors
- recent community/area change patterns
- financial resource issues
- population characteristics
- community attitude toward learning
- other issues pertinent to your community/school

Note: These factors are only considered to the degree that they may impact student performance.

Source: Corson, (2002). *Data Sources in Schools*. Used with permission. http://edservices.aea7.k12.ia.us/sibd/data/datasource.html.

Data can be collected through such methods and means as indicated in Figure 5.8.

Figure 5.8. Data Collection

Method	Purpose	End Product
Direct Observation	To see firsthand teaching, interaction patterns, behavior in the setting.	Fieldnotes, summaries.
Artifact Collection	To see products generated by students, teachers, other members of the school.	Summaries, packets with artifacts as illustrative cases of skill applications, and fieldnotes, tables, grade, or other types of distributions.
Surveys	To gather information from key stakeholders (teachers, parents, students, community members).	Analysis of data report.
Focus Groups	To gather information from select groups (parents, students, teachers).	Summary highlighting common themes.

Making Data User-Friendly

Although referring to the use of data in the school improvement process for system administrators, Togneri's (2003) suggestions about the quality and use of data are worthy of examination. District and, in turn, schools increase the likelihood that data will be used by:

♦ *Making the data safe.* Districts actively embrace data as a tool to help them improve. While districts celebrated positive data, leaders did not shy away from difficult information. They modeled acceptance of difficult data by pushing stakeholders to seek solutions rather than placing blame.

♦ *Making the data usable.* Districts also sought to provide school leaders to help interpret school-specific data. Still others provided technology to facilitate in-school disaggregation of data. Such tools allowed teachers and principals to get answers about trends within schools and to determine gaps in learning across certain groups of students.

♦ *Making use of the data.* Several districts did not simply provide data but also trained principals and teachers to use them. (p. 5, emphasis in the original)

Data Overload

Although school systems have technology to assist with generating data from multiple sources, too much data can cause data overload. Data overload is caused not only by the amount of data available to school systems but also if people do not understand how to use and interpret data. Chapter 6 gives a detailed description of what one principal did to make data user-friendly and also what this principal did to avoid data overload on the teachers.

Relative to the school improvement process, here are a few suggestions to help the principal prevent data overload:

♦ Present data related to showing the gaps in student performance in small increments.

♦ Ensure that data are presented in an easily read manner using graphs, charts, and other pictorials to illustrate numbers.

♦ Examine only one or two data sets at a time.

♦ Avoid presenting large amounts of data at the end of the day after teachers have spent a full day teaching.

♦ Enlist the support of district experts to assist in presenting and interpreting data. Local universities and colleges can also provide assistance.

Develop Improvement Goals and Objectives to Narrow Gaps

Goals

After analyzing data from various sources and considering the gaps identified, school improvement teams are ready to develop goals and objectives as a means to work strategies to address and hopefully to narrow gaps. "Goals are established based on the identified strengths and weaknesses of the school community to which school improvement activities will be directed. Goals are established to eliminate or minimize weaknesses and to enhance strength" (Indiana Department of Education, 2002, p. 11). When writing school improvement goals, they should be S.M.A.R.T:

♦ Specific

♦ Measurable

- ◆ Attainable

- ◆ Realistic (results-oriented)

- ◆ Time bound

The following are characteristics of well-developed goals focused on school improvement:

- ◆ Goals are primarily student-oriented. They describe what happens with and for students.

- ◆ Goals support the school mission statement.

- ◆ Goals describe the desired results rather than processes or strategies. They do not focus on quick fixes; that is the role of strategies.

- ◆ Goals are not buyable with dollars, because they describe how students benefit from qualitative change, not how facilities and resources are to be addressed.

- ◆ Goals stated in present tense with powerful verbs assist members of the school community as they describe the desired situation as if it were in place. (Indiana Department of Education, 2002, pp. 11–12)

Objectives

Closely related to goals are objectives. Whereas goals are generally broader, objectives are more specific, focusing efforts by

- ◆ Identifying a target population

- ◆ Identifying the assessments and the data sources that will be used to meet the objective

- ◆ Specifying anticipated progress anticipated

- ◆ Including short-term benchmarks (short-term check points) or standards that will be used to determine progress toward the achievement of the objective

Linking Goals and Objectives

The following illustrates the relationship of goals and objectives.

Goal: Increase student performance in the area of reading (the goal is purposefully broad and has no measurable standard).

Objective: "The percentage of students achieving the reading comprehension standard will increase from 50 to 60 by spring 2002 as measured by the state reading assessment exam at each grade level" (Bernhardt, 2002, p. 120).

Bernhardt (2002) recommends tracking information and the following tracking form (Figure 5.9) can assist the school improvement team in bringing order to the work of setting goals and objectives.

Figure 5.9. Tracking Goal Setting

Goal	Objective (Targets)	Resources Needed	Strategies	Assessment	Responsibility	Anticipated Time Frame

Develop Strategies to Meet Goals and Objectives

Once goals and objectives have been established, the school improvement team *and* all teachers need to work at developing strategies to help students and teachers meet the needs inherent in the goals and objectives. One way to develop strategies is to make this process a two-step one in which (1) the school improvement team develops a preliminary series of strategies and then (2) the school improvement team cast the net by getting input from the entire school. The school improvement team could present to the faculty strategies like this (Figure 5.10, p. 104).

Figure 5.10. Developing Strategies

Team_____   Grade_____

Subject/Content Area_____

Skill Focus_____

Identified gap:

Based on data sources:

Goals to close the gap:

Objectives to meet the goals to close the gap:

Targeted strategies to meet goals and objectives:

Resources needed to implement strategies:

Support needed from the principal, central office, or others to implement strategies:

Follow-up plans: (time frame, personnel)

Additional data sources needed:

Source: Adapted from *Target Area Worksheet for Lindsey Elementary School*. Houston County, Warner Robins, Georgia. Used with permission.

For the principal, this is a key area to focus support and resources so that teachers can implement strategies (the focus of the next chapter). Teachers will need time to meet in large and small groups. Small-group meetings would include grade level and subject area teachers. Larger group meeting time would include whole-school meetings. The principal can assist teachers in planning for these types of meetings and deliberations by ensuring that uninterrupted time during the day is provided (i.e., plan time). The principal needs to look for ways to manipulate the school day and the use of substitute teachers, paraprofessionals, and others to free teachers to work together in small and large groups.

The principal should anticipate *storming* and *norming* (see Chapter 4) as teachers work at developing strategies, because in an indirect way, the process is really asking for people to examine existing instructional practices that may or may not be working. Moreover, by developing or perhaps refining existing strategies and then moving to implement them, teachers are being asked to make changes that can cause pain and strain.

Corson (2000) provides a series of questions that can be asked to help guide the principal in examining and assessing both the strategies identified and the process of developing strategies:

- Are the strategies congruent with your values and beliefs?

- Do your strategies focus on systems improvement?

- Are the strategies within your scope of control?

- Was their consensus that the strategies are the best way to close the gap?

- Are there people assigned to key roles and responsibilities?

- Are the resources specifically identified?

Source: http://edservices.aea7.k12.ia.us/sibd/plans/actionplans.html.

The Action Plan is the School Improvement Plan

Action Plans Bring Life to Goals, Objectives, and Strategies

Action plans bring life to goals, objectives, and strategies, and action plans keep school improvement efforts moving forward. Often the information in an action plan includes information related to

- People responsible for implementing strategies

- Timelines for beginning and completing strategies

- Resources needed to implement strategies

- Potential barriers to successful implementation of strategies

- Possible prevention of barriers

- Evaluation procedures for acknowledging successful realization of strategies

- Activities to celebrate successes. (Indiana Department of Education, 2002, p. 13)

"The...school improvement plan...is NOT an end in itself. The Plan is a MEANS to an end" (North Carolina State Department of Public Education, 1999, p. 150). School improvement plans codify what is important:

- Unifying school improvement efforts from all parts of the school community

♦ Providing a road map for implementing school improvement efforts

♦ Communicating to the school community of the specific direction school improvement is taking

Pulling It All Together— A Case from the Field

R.W. Lindsey Elementary School
81 Tabor Drive
Warner Robins, GA 31093
Dr. Ruth O'Dell, Principal
(478) 929–7818 (Phone)
(478) 542–2296 (Fax)
rodell@hcbe.net

Dr. Mike Mattingly
Executive Director of Elementary Operations
Houston County Schools
Houston County, GA

The following case is condensed from four years of work that Dr. Ruth O'Dell and her staff tackled to bring about schoolwide improvement. The value of this case study is found in the process of planning that was used in the school improvement process. The reader is encouraged to reflect not only on the process factors involved in the following case but also on aspects such as culture and climate (Chapter 2), teacher leadership (Chapter 3), and team building (Chapter 4) needed to bring about school improvement. Dr. O'Dell stresses that no single strategy will work to bring about school improvement, but that school improvement emerges when a school and its community can incorporate a series of strategies.

R. W. Lindsey Elementary School in Warner Robins, Georgia (Houston County Schools), is a Title I school that has beat remarkable odds by moving from a low-performing, needs-improvement status to a Title I performing school. This move in status was no accident. The change was a direct result of the commitment of faculty who worked incredibly hard to take school improvement seriously, according to principal, Dr. Ruth O'Dell. She became principal of Lindsey Elementary School in 1999 after a succession of changes in leadership. Several strategies that O'Dell implemented in the school improvement process mirror best practices for the work needed to shepherd school and community through the changes necessary to move from a low-performing school to a school that performs.

Understanding the Context

Built in 1954, R. W. Lindsey Elementary School, serves approximately 367 prekindergarten through fifth-grade students, of whom 88 percent are participating in the free or reduced lunch program (the overall district rate of students eligible to receive free and reduced lunches is 38 percent). The ethnicity of students includes 86 percent African American; 13 percent white; and 1 percent other. Approximately 98 percent of the students are minority, and students are highly transient with data suggesting that during the first semester of 1999, 50 children withdrew from Lindsey Elementary and 75 new students enrolled.

Lindsey Elementary houses a full-day prekindergarten and regular kindergarten programs as well as a special education class. A comparison of school district averages of poverty level and minority representation reveal that Lindsey has the highest poverty and minority population in the school district.

Academic Support Programs and Personnel

The socioeconomic level of the surrounding community in which students reside qualifies Lindsey to provide services through a schoolwide Title I program and other remedial programs. For example, the Reading Recovery Program provides the school with two reading specialists. The program's goal is to bring students up to the level of their peers and to give students the assistance they need to develop independent reading strategies.

Schoolwide Title I funds provide a certified teacher to act as a part-time parent coordinator. In addition to providing classroom instruction three days a week, this teacher serves as a school–community liaison. The responsibilities include identifying and locating community resources to help children and their families better resolve family problems. The parent coordinator also tutors parents and children on specifics that may be blocking progress in school and areas of personal development. In addition, the parent coordinator contacts parents regarding volunteer assistance, plans parenting workshops, coordinates the parent resource room, makes home visits, and orients parents to volunteer activities.

The Faculty of Lindsey Elementary

There are 41 teachers at Lindsey Elementary: 30 percent African American and 68 percent white. Fifteen paraprofessionals provide support services. The administrative staff consists of a principal, assistant principal, and a counselor. Lindsey Elementary also has a family literacy coordinator, a literacy coordinator, a media specialist, and a part-time instructional coach.

The Reality of a School in Trouble

Test scores from 1996 to 1999 placed Lindsey Elementary in the Title I category of *Needs Improvement, Not Progressing*. Data from the Council of School Performance indicated that Lindsey Elementary was in the bottom 20 percent of schools with similar profiles of high poverty.

Scanning the Environment

Because teacher morale and efficacy are so important to school improvement, O'Dell wanted to understand the community. Before officially beginning as principal, O'Dell took the approach that she had to scan the environment to understand the culture, climate, and unique characteristics of students, teachers, parents, and the community and its members whom Lindsey Elementary serves. To do this, O'Dell spent several half-days at Lindsey Elementary, met with teachers who could "break away" during the summer, and surveyed teachers and parents. O'Dell took a broad approach to the design of the survey that she administered to teachers. She asked teachers to "list 3 or 4 strengths and weaknesses" at Lindsey Elementary School. O'Dell wanted to know what teachers believed were the most pressing needs. Across the board, data indicated:

- *Discipline*: Students were out of control.
- *Facility and housekeeping*: The school's physical plant was not clean.
- *Low parental involvement*: Parents only came to the school when there was a problem.
- *Teacher participation and morale were low*: Teachers felt that they were not listened to.
- *Lack of communication and organizational planning.*
- *Curriculum and instruction were not aligned* to the characteristics of the students served by Lindsey Elementary School.
- *Student motivation to learn was low.*

In a follow-up meeting with teachers, O'Dell shared these results and asked teachers to rank the weaknesses of Lindsey Elementary because she wanted to begin the process of "turning things around" from an organizational level so that the school could move into the work of increasing student learning. O'Dell believed that she could not start the work of school improvement and strengthening the academic program until the patterns of organizational support were in place. O'Dell also knew that until discipline had improved and a more positive school climate had been established, that no efforts, no matter how small or big, would bring about school improvement relative to student achievement.

The next step of the scanning process involved meeting with teachers to see how they wanted "to organize" to work. In the end, teachers decided that they wanted to organize by grade level and across subject areas. O'Dell also began to develop teams, including a governance team, which could be empowered to help lead the school toward school improvement. This team included O'Dell, the assistant principal, and the school counselor. After examining the results of the survey and feedback from teachers, the consensus was to narrow the list of weaknesses to address

♦ Lack of parent support

♦ Lack of teamwork between grade levels

♦ Unclean learning environment

O'Dell also wanted to gain the perspectives of parents, and she planned three "Drop-in Parent Forums." The forums lasted approximately two hours (6:00 to 8:00 P.M.), and the format included small group discussions facilitated by O'Dell, the assistant principal, the school counselor, and the parent coordinator. Refreshments and childcare were offered. Each parent was asked to complete an open-ended survey.

Parent Survey

Please complete this survey and return to your child's teacher. You may also bring it to the Parent Forum on Thursday. *We would love to see you at Lindsey!!!*

1. How do you think we could get more parents involved at Lindsey?

2. How welcome do you feel at Lindsey? How might we improve in this area?

3. How might we improve the home–school relationship at Lindsey? What might teachers do? What could parents do?

4. Do you feel your child is learning what he/she needs to learn at Lindsey? If not, what areas need improving?

Results were analyzed across three broad questions:

1. What keeps parents from getting involved at Lindsey?

   • Background checks

   • Working parents

   • Single parents

   • Transportation

- Effective parent programs
- "Discomfort" about coming to school
- Lack of teacher commitment and participation

2. How can we get more parents involved at Lindsey?

- More parent-teacher-family social activities (pot lucks, hay rides, sporting activities)
- Talent show was a big interest to parents
- Regular speakers/workshops of interest to parents (once a month)
- More plays and programs where parents see their children participate
- Get churches and pastors involved
- Events held right after school
- More exposure to what their children are learning (new math, reading)
- Send home constant reminders on how parents can be more involved
- Personal contact from teachers: calls home and home visits
- Rewards for 100 percent participation
- After-school program every day
- Home visits
- Teachers getting involved with students and their families
- Treating parents with respect, "not talking down to them"
- Offer more volunteer positions for parents
- Send more projects home that require parent involvement

3. Do parents feel welcome at Lindsey?

The vast majority of the surveys indicated that parents feel very welcome at the school. One person mentioned keeping the doors "locked to parents" at 3:00, and another mentioned the need for more positive attitudes on the part of teachers.

Where to Start?

The needs of Lindsey Elementary were many, and student achievement data put the students performing at the lowest quartile in Houston County and the state. There was much work to be accomplished, and O'Dell knew that it would take many years to help the teachers turn things around at Lindsey Elementary. All the necessary ingredients were present—a dedicated cadre of teachers and other school personnel, concerned parents, and a supportive central administration and board of education, yet achievement was elusive. Also elusive to faculty was the norm of working with one another on behalf of students and community.

In September 1999, school improvement became the focus of faculty meetings, biweekly grade-level meetings, cross-grade-level meetings, grade chair meetings, Shared Decision Team Meetings, and parental involvement meetings. The priority was to make Lindsey Elementary a school in which academic, social, and emotional learning would occur for teachers, students, and parents.

Teamwork—Time, Opportunity, and Training Needed

O'Dell worked with teachers so that they would become the "planners of school improvement," and she worked with teachers in developing shared decision making so that teachers could begin to address the real issues that were standing in the way of students being able to be successful learners.

One of O'Dell's goals centered on building capacity for teachers, and she wanted to provide the support and the structure needed to prompt teacher and staff leadership (see Chapter 3). A perception of a lack of teamwork between grade levels troubled O'Dell the most, in that it appeared that teachers did not work well with one another, not because they did not want to, but rather because they had not been given the opportunity or training on how to work toward a common goal (see Chapter 4). O'Dell believed that "her" teachers were dedicated to the children—they just needed the time, opportunity, and support to work with one another. O'Dell believed that giving teachers a voice in how they could work with one another would only begin by having a common vision and mission at Lindsey Elementary School (see Chapter 2).

O'Dell also realized that there was not a coordinated way in which teachers could meet to discuss issues, and there was no formal structure to involve teachers in schoolwide decision making and problem solving, and that when teams did meet, there was no way for teams to communicate needs to her. O'Dell worked with Lindsey faculty and staff to implement a shared decision-making model.

Developing the structure for the shared decision-making team took almost three years of experimentation for O'Dell and the Lindsey faculty and staff. Planning for this structure included first establishing grade-level teams, Jet Teams, in which a chair from each Jet Team would meet with O'Dell, the assistant principal, and the instructional coordinator. Issues during the first year included a focus on bolstering teacher morale and examining gaps in student learning and what support was needed to help teachers examine their instructional practices.

Given the immediacy of the work that needed to be accomplished, much of the time at these meetings dealt with "putting out fires," and the development of quick fixes to the immediate problem rather than long-term planning and building of strategies. O'Dell saw a need to extend the structure of the Jet Teams into a more formal decision-making body—shared problem solving and decision making.

As teachers became more comfortable with being part of the decision-making process, O'Dell made the shift by developing decision teams. Each Jet Team chose one person that would serve as a member for the Operations/Personnel, Instructional Chairs, and Student/Parent Support decision team.

Operations/Personnel	*Instructional Chairs*	*Student/Parent Support*
Budget/Finance School Beautification Teacher Morale Communication	Instructional Issues Media and Technology Accelerated Reader Professional Development	Student Support Team Process Discipline/School Climate Parental Involvement Guidance/Character Education ISS/Alternative Program

Jet Teams met once a week during planning time, or before or after school, and O'Dell requested that the Jet Teams develop their meeting schedule for the year by the end of the first week of the school year.

Decision Teams met once a month after school with the following ground rules:

♦ Any faculty or staff member can put items on the agendas. Input boxes for each Decision Team were placed in the teacher workroom.

♦ Decision Team Chairs will develop the agenda for these meetings and facilitate the meetings.

♦ Decision Teams may appoint ad hoc committees at times when more information or study is needed.

O'Dell worked with the central office to find a way to compensate Decision Team members, and she was able to secure a $100 stipend and secure one staff development unit (SDU) credit for the Decision Team members for reading and studying issues (including research) that would be part of the work of team members.

By the end of the third year, the Decision Teams were addressing the issues that related to the school being able to move in a direction of improvement, and teachers were actively involved in the process working alongside the administration in making and implementing decisions. During the third year, the Decision Teams accomplished a great deal to enhance the learning environment, and the work of these teams focused the efforts of the administration team in providing the support teachers and staff needed.

Mission

During 1999–2000, the faculty and staff of Lindsey Elementary began the school improvement process, and O'Dell worked with the teachers to develop a mission that would "hold the vision" for what students were capable of working toward—achievement and learning that was developmentally appropriate. O'Dell and the faculty spent three full faculty meetings and a half-day retreat discussing the roles of teachers, students, and parents in improving the educational status of children. After brainstorming all the beliefs held about what Lindsey Elementary should seek to accomplish, a committee was appointed to take all the input and to craft a mission that best reflected the beliefs of the school and community.

As part of the self-study, the mission was revisited. A subcommittee reviewed the mission and found it to be very consistent with the beliefs and behavior of Lindsey Elementary faculty and staff. The committee believed that the mission could provide guidance in making decisions and allowed everyone to visualize the purpose of the efforts at Lindsey Elementary.

Mission Statement
Lindsey Elementary School

The purpose and goal of Lindsey Elementary is to promote a supportive and challenging learning environment by creating bridges between the school, the community, and students. We envision meeting the needs of the whole child: mentally, physically, academically, and emotionally. Given the necessary resources from the community and school system, we can work collaboratively to create an atmosphere that motivates students, parents, and faculty to become productive lifelong learners.

The word *productive* was added in describing learners, and the recommendation was made that the mission be posted "everywhere in the school" to remind everyone of the purpose for being at Lindsey Elementary. The mission and belief statements were published and disseminated by way of posters in the teacher workroom and classrooms, parent newsletters, the school Web site, and brochures about Lindsey Elementary (see Chapter 2).

Beliefs = Values Forms the Basis of the Mission

Faculty participated further in developing the beliefs of the school by completing the Beliefs Survey provided by the National Study of School Evaluation (NSSE). These data were examined to find common patterns and ideas about the beliefs of the Lindsey Elementary faculty. A cross section of parents met with O'Dell to discuss their perceptions and beliefs about Lindsey Elementary. The parents expressed their beliefs:

- ◆ In the importance of home–parent communication
- ◆ Ongoing professional development for teachers
- ◆ The involvement of parents in the education of their children
- ◆ Concern over the motivation level of their children

O'Dell reported that the expectations expressed in the meetings with the parents were consistent with those developed by the faculty and staff.

Committing the Beliefs of Faculty, Staff, Administration, and Parents to Writing

- ◆ Students learn in different ways and should be provided with a variety of instructional approaches to support their learning.
- ◆ Students learn best when they are actively engaged in the learning process.
- ◆ Each student is a valued individual with unique physical, social, emotional, and intellectual needs.
- ◆ A safe and physically comfortable environment promotes student learning.
- ◆ Schools need to function as a learning organization and promote opportunities for all those who have a stake in the success of the school to work together as a community of learners.
- ◆ The commitment to continuous improvements is imperative if our school is going to enable students to become confident, self-directed, lifelong learners.

Gap Analysis—The Current Reality versus the Desired State

By examining perceptions as reported in data from past accreditation reports, polling faculty, and consulting trends (class size, curriculum guides), the following challenges were reported by the teachers as barriers to success:

♦ Low performance on standardized tests (see data set from 1999 in Figures 5.13 to 5.15, pp. 124–125).

♦ Too many students in classrooms.

♦ Understanding at-risk students and students from poverty (88 percent of Lindsey students participate in the free and reduced lunch programs).

♦ Too many students are not on grade level in reading and math.

♦ Curriculum needs to be more appropriate to our school.

♦ Curriculum needs to be more consistent from grade to grade.

♦ Staff development to improve teaching skills.

♦ Staff development in guided reading/literacy.

♦ Lack of materials when we get new series adoptions.

♦ We need to believe these students can improve.

Test Data Analysis and Discussion in and across Grade Levels

Data from tests and discussion in and across grade levels uncovered similar findings as inherent in survey of perceptions and whole-school discussions. The following is a summary of challenges:

♦ Lack of basic skills in reading and math

♦ Lack of comprehension and reasoning skills in reading and math

♦ Lack of "word attack" skills

♦ Difficulty taking standardized tests

♦ Lack of writing [including handwriting] skills

♦ Lack of motivation to achieve

An Overall Reform Strategy

Given the beliefs and mission, O'Dell slowly began to introduce the principles included in the Comer School Development Model:

To realize the full potential of schools and students, we must create—and adequately support—a wide and deep pool of teachers and administrators who, in addition to having thorough knowledge of their disciplines, know how children develop generally and academically and how to support that development. They must be able to engage the families of students and the institutions and people in communities in a way that benefits student growth in school and society. (Comer, 2001, p. 8)

The principles of the Comer School Development Program (Figure 5.11) were appealing to the Lindsey Elementary community.

Figure 5.11. The Comer School Development Program

WHAT IS IT?

♦ James Comer's School Development Program, also known as the Comer Process, is intended to improve the educational experience of poor minority youth. Improvement is attained by building supportive bonds among children, parents, and school staff *to promote a positive school climate*.

WHAT ARE ITS GOALS?

♦ The School Development Program is designed to create a school environment where children feel comfortable, valued, and secure. In this environment, children will form positive emotional bonds with school staff and parents and a positive attitude toward the school program, which promotes the children's overall development and, in turn, facilitates academic learning.

WHAT ARE ITS PRINCIPLES?

♦ Three principles underlie the Comer Process:
  • Schools must review problems in open discussion in a *no-fault* atmosphere;
  • Each school must develop *collaborative working relationships* among principals, parents, teachers, community leaders, superintendents, and health-care workers; and
  • All decisions must be reached by *consensus* rather than by decree.

HOW DOES IT WORK?

♦ The School Development Program relies on staff collaboration and parent involvement to promote expectations of high student achievement. Each Comer school implements the program differently depending on the personalities of its staff and the specific needs of the school and its students.

♦ Each Comer school is governed by the following three teams:

- The School Planning and Management Team. This building-level governing and management body is headed by the principal and comprises teachers, administrators, parents, support staff, and a child development specialist. As a team they are responsible for identifying targets for social and academic improvement, establishing policy guidelines, developing systematic school plans, responding to problems, and monitoring program activities.

- The Mental Health Team. This team is headed by the principal and includes teachers, administrators, psychologists, social workers, and nurses. Together they analyze social and behavioral patterns within the school and determine how to solve recurring problems, applying child development principles in their decision making.

- The Parents' Group. The goal of this group is to involve parents in all levels of school activity, from volunteering in the classroom to school governance.

Source: U.S. Department of Education (1993). *Office of Research Education Consumer Guide: The Comer School Development Program.* http://www.ed.gov/pubs/OR/ ConsumerGuides/comer.html.

As a former school counselor with a background in childhood psychology, O'Dell knew the power of a model grounded in principles that would help in meeting children's psychological and social needs through developmentally appropriate approaches to learning, parental involvement, and an absolute belief that students at Lindsey Elementary can learn.

O'Dell's approach to leadership was guided by three key principles, as reported by Cook, Hunt, and Murphy (1998):

♦ Adult groups should cooperate with each other and always put student needs above their own. The assumption is that competing adults do not have the focus or energy required to serve children well.

- All adults in the building should adopt a problem-solving rather than a fault-finding orientation. This avoids counterproductive acrimony and fosters improved teamwork.

- Decision making by consensus rather than vote or principal fiat . . . requires listening to others and developing empathy for others' views.

- Once these three process principles are dominant in a school, Comer believes that the staff will then focus on attaining widely shared goals, interpersonal trust will be a premier building norm, and local children's needs will be well understood and obviously paramount. A more humane and effective school should result from all of this.

Databased Decision Making and Planning for Change

The work accomplished during 1999 (mission, beliefs, team development, outreach to parents, and gap analysis) paved the way for the school to tackle issues related to curriculum and instruction in 2000. Teachers across and within grade levels, along with paraprofessionals and other Lindsey Elementary staff, worked toward developing a more "focused" curriculum based on research that shows that "less is more" for at-risk students. O'Dell and her faculty and staff spent two days in the summer reviewing the Quality Core Curriculum (QCC), results from the Iowa Basic Skills, and the Criterion Referenced Test Standards. Based on this review, each of the QCC objectives were labeled as *Essential*, *Important*, or *Nonessential* for Lindsey Elementary students.

The faculty decided to use all the components of a Balanced Literacy program in grades K–5 to create a literacy rich environment for students to include the following strategies:

Read Aloud	Shared Writing
Shared Reading	Interactive Writing
Guided Reading	Guided Writing
Independent Reading	Independent Writing
Phonics/Word Matters	Phonics/Word Matters

Using Figure 5.10 (see p. 104), O'Dell and her faculty by grade level, agreed on the following areas, goals, and strategies to create a Balanced Literacy Program:

Balanced Literacy Areas of Focus for Each Grade

- Pre-K through first grade:
  - Read-a-Louds
  - Shared/interactive writing
  - Modeling reading
  - Comprehension

- Ssecond grade:
  - Writing workshop
  - Reading comprehension strategies
  - "Word matters" skills that will foster the transition to third grade

- Third grade:
  - Working with words/word matters
  - Writing workshop
  - Reading comprehension strategies

- Fourth and fifth grades:
  - Reading comprehension (higher-order thinking levels)
  - Reading comprehension in content areas

A commitment was made by the teachers and O'Dell to

- Provide ongoing staff development in teaching writing and reading comprehension.
- Reinforce test-taking strategies every Friday schoolwide.
- Continue and refine the Accelerated Reader Program.
- Continue after-school program.
- Continue to add significantly to our book room, library, and classroom libraries, especially nonfiction material and short texts that are more easily used for reading comprehension instruction.

Academic Goals—
Something to Strive For

The following goals were set by the Lindsey Elementary faculty:

Reading Goals

- The average NCE score on the ITBS in Total Reading will improve by 5 points schoolwide.

- The percentage of students scoring below the 40th percentile on the ITBS in Total Reading will be reduced by 8 percent.

- Ninety percent of students will exhibit 80 percent accuracy on comprehension questions (including higher order reasoning) at their text level by the end of each grade level.

- Ninety percent of students will exhibit 80 percent accuracy of Dolch basic sight words at the end of each grade level.

Writing Goals

- Ninety percent of students will write a passage that includes main idea, supporting details, and a conclusion at an adequate level by the end of the third grade.

- Ninety percent of students will write a passage with correct spelling, grammar, and punctuation at an adequate level by the end of third grade.

- Ninety percent of students will print legibly by end of first grade.

- Ninety percent of students will use cursive writing legibly by end of fourth grade.

Math Goals

- The average NCE score on the ITBS in Total Math will increase by 5 points.

- The percentage of students scoring below the 40th percentile on the ITBS in Total Math will be reduced by 8 percent.

- Eighty-five percent of students will exhibit 95 percent accuracy on basic math facts in addition and subtraction by the end of the third grade.

- Eighty-five percent of students will exhibit 95 percent accuracy on basic math facts in multiplication and division by the end of third grade.

- Ninety percent of students will solve a two-step word problem by the end of the third grade.

- Ninety percent of students will solve a three-step word problem by the end of the fifth grade.

- Ninety percent of students at each grade level will be able to analyze charts and diagrams at their grade level.

Student Behavior/Motivation

♦ One hundred percent of students in grades K–2 will complete daily homework folders and homework assignments.

♦ One hundred percent of students in grades 3–5 will complete daily agendas and homework assignments.

Student Behavior/Discipline

♦ Reduce by 20 percent the percentage of students assigned to ISS.

♦ Increase by 20 percent the participation in GBAs.

Parental Involvement

♦ Increase to 50 percent the individual involvement of parents in their child's education.

♦ Increase to 40 percent attendance of parents at PTO meetings.

Ongoing Assessment

A comprehensive assessment system was developed by Lindsey teachers and included six-week assessments, mid-year assessments, and end-of-year assessments. Running records of student progress were used continuously. The Houston County Literacy Inventory was used in kindergarten, first, and second grade. The GKAP-R was used in kindergarten. The AR program provided ongoing assessments for children in grades 2 through 5. O'Dell asked the faculty to consider two questions:

1. What schoolwide strategies are working?

2. What should we do between now and the end of the year?

The Research Base Needed to Press Forward

O'Dell and her teachers consulted the research base to assist in the development of strategies:

Exemplary Practices of Teachers

♦ Essential questions.

♦ Graphic organizers.

♦ Vocabulary emphasis.

♦ Unit planning.

♦ Higher-order cognitive strategies.

♦ Hit all three levels of learning.

**Components of Effective
Research-Based Literacy Program**

- Minimum of 2–3 hours or reading and writing instruction per day.

- Instruction must emphasize four equally important framework components.

- Supervision must be linked to the framework.

- Continuity matters (consistent and pervasive).

- Professional development is essential.

**Reading Comprehension
and Higher-Order Thinking**

- Direct instruction of strategies

- Determining important information

- Authentic evidence of student learning

Strategies to Implement the Research

O'Dell, taking the lead with Lindsey Elementary faculty, made the commitment shown in Figure 5.12 to keep the press on student achievement and school improvement moving forward.

Figure 5.12. Lindsey Organization 2003–2004

- 8:30–11:00 Literacy block for everyone

- Absolutely no interruptions!

- Lindsey curriculum guide: consistent and pervasive

- Quarterly benchmark assessment

- Vertical teaming

- Planning vertically and on grade levels

- Professional development aligned with the framework: coaching, modeling, taping, feedback, independent reading, support

- Supervision aligned with the framework

- Accountability shared by all: no grouping

- All personnel working with students at all times

- Revamp after-school program

Strategies to Increase Parental Involvement

The mission statement served as a means for the Lindsey Elementary community to start the process of building bridges between students, parents, and teachers. The faculty from grade levels, the literacy coach, and parent coordinator helped to shape the policies and strategies to involve parents in the education of their child.

- Teachers will have at least two parent conferences per child in their homeroom class. One will be within the first two months of school; and one, after the Christmas break and before the Easter break.

- Each K–5 student will be given agenda/homework folder at the beginning of the school year. This will be used as one method of promoting home–school communication.

- Teachers will send home one "positive note" per student each six weeks.

- The school will investigate the possibility of cell phones or cordless phones for each grade level.

O'Dell adapted strategies to promote home–school contact beyond that of the teachers. As a school, Lindsey Elementary developed the following:

- All PTO meetings will provide meals, childcare, and one performance by grade level.

- "Dynamite" door prizes at each event.

- Each grade level will host a parent forum/workshop every six weeks per year.

- Have an interactive Back to School Night.

- Sponsor three parent "social events" per year: Fall Festival, Talent Night, Field Day.

- Parents will be personally invited to attend meetings with phone calls and postcards.

- Each homeroom will have a homeroom parent who will assist with bulletin boards and activities such as calling parents and field trips.

- Investigate the background check process and seek some modifications.

Data Say It All

What were the results of the efforts of the Lindsey faculty? Figures 5.13 through 5.15 landscape the remarkable improvements of this school. The people who work at Lindsey Elementary are "Jets" who have been able to spark the support and enthusiasm of students and parents.

Figure 5.13. Lindsey Elementary Fourth-Grade CRCT Reading Data

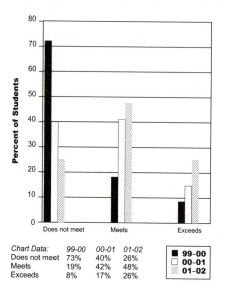

Chart Data:	99-00	00-01	01-02
Does not meet	73%	40%	26%
Meets	19%	42%	48%
Exceeds	8%	17%	26%

■ 99–00
□ 00–01
▨ 01–02

Figure 5.14. Lindsey Elementary Fourth-Grade CRCT Language Arts Data

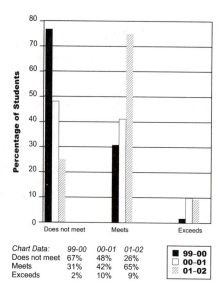

Chart Data:	99-00	00-01	01-02
Does not meet	67%	48%	26%
Meets	31%	42%	65%
Exceeds	2%	10%	9%

■ 99–00
□ 00–01
▨ 01–02

Figure 5.15. Lindsey Elementary Fourth-Grade CRCT Mathematics Data

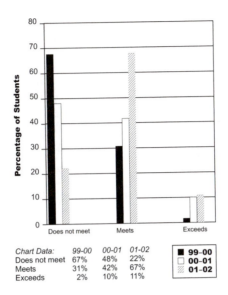

Chart Data:	99-00	00-01	01-02
Does not meet	67%	48%	22%
Meets	31%	42%	67%
Exceeds	2%	10%	11%

■ 99-00
□ 00-01
▨ 01-02

Suggested Readings

Bernhardt, V. L. (2002). *The school portfolio toolkit: A planning, implementation, and evaluation guide for continuous school improvement*. Larchmont, NY: Eye on Education.

Chenoweth, T. G., & Everhart, R. B. (2002). *Navigating comprehensive school change: A guide for the perplexed*. Larchmont, NY: Eye on Education.

Choo, C. W. (2001). Environmental scanning as information seeking and organizational learning. *Information Research, 7*(1). Retrieved July 27, 2003, from http://www.informationr.net/ir/7-1/paper112.html.

Comer, J. P., Haynes, N. M., Joyner, E. T., & Ben-Avie, M. B. (1996). *Rallying the whole village: The Comer process for reforming education*. New York: Teachers College Press.

Elmore, R. F. (2002). *Bridging the gap between standards and achievement: The imperative for professional development in education*. Washington, DC: Albert Shanker Institute.

The Education Quality and Accountability Office. (2000). *Ontario report and guide on school improvement planning: 1999–2000*. Retrieved from http://www.eqao.com/eqao/home_page/pdf_e/00/00P056e.pdf

Togneri, W. (2003). *Beyond islands of excellence: What districts can do to improve instruction and achievement in all schools—A leadership brief*. Washington, DC: Learning First Alliance.

Zepeda, S. J. (2003). *The principal as instructional leader: A handbook for supervisors*. Larchmont, NY: Eye on Education.

6

The Work of the Principal in Implementing and Monitoring School Improvement

In this Chapter…

- ♦ Implementing school improvement plans
- ♦ Professional development needed for successful implementation
- ♦ Characteristics of effective professional development
- ♦ Monitoring school improvement
- ♦ Understanding data—A precursor to reviewing efforts and modifying goals, objectives, and strategies
- ♦ Sustaining the momentum for school improvement

Implementing School Improvement

Implementing the school improvement plan takes a commitment to working with teachers—it is that simple but complex in that there are many interrelated processes involved with implementation of school improvement. According to Van Heusden Hale (2000),

> implementation begins when you reach a point where you are confident about what needs to happen to improve your school. Successful implementation does not have a definitive beginning and end; nor is it typically a linear process. It depends a lot on the rigor and sound-

ness of the school reform approach, the motivation of the individuals involved, and the accuracy of the needs your team has identified. In fact, implementation is a continuous cycle of planning, taking action, evaluating, and adjusting course, if necessary, that permeates any successful reform effort and guides future actions. (p. 50)

Implementation begins by keeping an eye on the desired end state and by asking questions such as

- What gaps have been identified?

- What strategies need to be implemented to remediate the gaps?

- How do people ready to make changes?

For the principal, overseeing the process of school improvement plans consists of several ongoing activities, including

- Implementing the plan

- Providing staff development to help teachers carry out the school improvement efforts

- Documenting results

- Reviewing efforts and results of achieving goals within the school improvement plan

- Modifying goals and strategies needed to reach improvement

- Rethinking what works and what does not seem to be working in a fault-free manner

- Requesting help from beyond the school walls, including learning from others and partnerships with other entities

- Exploring what is blocking progress toward meeting goals

- Sustaining the commitment to continuous improvement.

These activities are covered in this chapter as a means to assist the principal and others in achieving schoolwide improvement goals and objectives. The principal and the school improvement team need to develop a plan to provide teachers and others with professional development opportunities and other resources to meet the objectives of school improvement. Resources can range from inservice with follow-up coaching to off-site observations of teachers who use a particular strategy. Professional development is a prerequisite to implementation of strategies, as many new strategies go beyond doing things differently. *A Report of the National Partnership for Excellence and Accountability in Teaching* (National Partnership for Excellence and Accountability in Teaching, 1999b), indicates the need for a learning-centered approach for both teachers and students:

School improvement and learner-centered professional development go hand in hand. Education reform that makes a difference for students requires teachers and principals to respond in new ways to the need for change and to rebuild the very foundation of their thinking about teaching and learning. (p. 2)

Closely related to implementation is monitoring the results of school improvement efforts. Monitoring can take many forms (observations, tracking student progress through test scores, portfolios). Monitoring the results of school improvement efforts is an ongoing and formative process that relies on data from multiple sources. O'Dell (see Chapter 5, "Pulling It All Together—A Case from the Field," p. 106) monitored the efforts of school improvement in her school continuously to include six-week assessments, mid-year assessments, and end-of-year assessments, and O'Dell did this to determine if people were "hitting the mark" toward improvement.

Teachers need to be the primary actors in monitoring the effects of school improvement strategies as they unfold in the classroom. The principal and other members of the leadership team need to work with teachers so that they can keep one eye on what they are doing and the other eye on the results of their efforts, asking: "Are children learning?"

O'Dell asked the faculty to consider two questions as they worked together to assess their individual and collective efforts:

- What schoolwide strategies are working?
- What should we do between now and the end of the year?

These questions and others answered through data will guide the monitoring process and will help teachers to make mid-course corrections if results are not leading them to the desired end result. The results derived through monitoring efforts link back to the school improvement processes of planning and implementing.

Implementing School Improvement Plans

Part of the school improvement planning process (Chapter 5) includes examining goals and objectives as a way to get to where you want to go (the desired state). Goals and objectives leading to the development of strategies pave the way for implementation.

After determining the desired state, members of the school community develop strategies aligned with the goals and objectives. Strategies are a way to address gaps and the obstacles that prevent reaching goals and objectives. Strategies are what guide people in making changes to the current situation and implementing school improvement. Taken further, implementation strategies and their results are what are monitored.

Implementing the Plan

Given the relative importance of strategy development related to the implementation of school improvement efforts in the classroom and initiatives more broadly across the school system, it is essential to understand underlying assumptions about them. According the Indiana Department of Education (2003) (IDE), "Strategies outline a variety of possible activities to achieve the goals of the school [511 IAC 6.1–7-1(c)(3)(D)]. Strategies are practical, manageable, and flexible enough to allow for modifications." Moreover, IDE identifies the characteristics of well-developed strategies (Figure 6.1).

Figure 6.1. Characteristics of Well-Developed Strategies

The following are characteristics of well-developed strategies:

♦ Strategies may emerge from the ideas and experiences of the participants, from best practices in the field, and professional literature.

♦ Each goal has its own set of strategies. Strategies may suggest a sequence of activities.

♦ Strategies are congruent with local and state policies.

♦ Strategies are action-oriented and clearly state various ways to implement the goal.

♦ Strategies provide justification for the allocation of time, money, and staff development needed to realize the goal.

♦ Strategies indicate how various members of the school community may be involved in implementation of the activities.

♦ Strategies realistically address changes which must occur to implement the goal.

♦ Strategies allow for ongoing evaluation. This evaluation may suggest additional strategies and refinement of goals.

Source: Indiana Department of Education—Division of Accountability (2003). *Suggested Approaches to School Improvement Planning*. http://ideanet.doe.state.in.us/accreditation/suppb.html.

Implementing strategies is the jumping-off point for school improvement. In sum, strategies describe possibilities for active progress toward the goals, and strategies lead people in implementing school improvement.

The principal's role in leading the school improvement process is pivotal. All resources, including the principal's time and energy, must be allocated to implementation of school improvement efforts. The following implementation suggestions (Figure 6.2) can act as a guide for the principal and school improvement team.

Figure 6.2. School Improvement Implementation Strategies

- ♦ Develop an implementation calendar and include activities and a time frame.

- ♦ Communicate expectations.

- ♦ Develop a staff development plan for the school related to the expectations of the school improvement plan.

- ♦ Collect successful strategies data from schools that have outperformed you in priority areas of need.

- ♦ Review research-based strategies that address your problem.

- ♦ Choose the strategies that you will implement to address your problem.

- ♦ Identify milestones for monitoring progress.

- ♦ Identify activities that will support the strategy.

- ♦ Identify people responsible for implementing strategies, collecting the assessment data, and monitoring overall progress.

Source: Adapted from "Implementing the Plan" and "Choosing Strategies" (n.d.), both from *School Improvement in Maryland.* http://www.mdk12.org/process/10steps/7/index.html and http://www.mdk12.org/process/10steps/6/index.html.

Professional Development Needed for Successful Implementation

What the principal makes time for sends a clear signal to the community of what is important. All programs—staff development, mentoring, induction, peer coaching—can assist the principal focus the attention of the school on improvement. Professional development is the primary vehicle for implementing school improvement efforts, as Joyce and Showers (2002) state:

Selecting the content of staff development is one of the most critical decisions in the school improvement process. If you are to attain your student achievement goals, the content of staff development needs to be aligned with those goals. And the content needs to be robust enough to effect the type of change envisioned. (p. 59)

Teachers need the opportunity and time to work with one another; they will learn more from sustained discussion on classroom practices, coaching opportunities, and the formal and informal mentoring they can provide to one another. Thompson (1992) believes that "school improvement demands recognition of the link between schooling and resource effects, and the result should be a model for school improvement which places staff development at the apex of priorities" (p. 174).

Related to school improvement, Section 9101(34) of the NCLB provides guidelines for staff development (Figure 6.3).

Figure 6.3. Professional Development Related to NCLB

Professional Development [Section 9101(34)]

The term *professional development*

1. Includes activities that
♦ Improve and increase teachers' knowledge of the academic subjects the teachers teach, and enable teachers to become highly qualified.

♦ Are an integral part of broad schoolwide and district-wide educational improvement plans.

♦ Give teachers, principals, and administrators the knowledge and skills to provide students with the opportunity to meet challenging state academic content standards and student academic achievement standards.

♦ Improve classroom management skills.

♦ Are high quality, sustained, intensive, and classroom-focused to have a positive and lasting impact on classroom instruction and the teacher's performance in the classroom and are not one-day or short-term workshops or conferences.

♦ Support the recruiting, hiring, and training of highly qualified teachers, including teachers who became highly qualified through state and local alternative routes to certification.

♦ Advance teacher understanding of effective instructional strategies that are
   • Based on scientifically based research (except that this subclause shall not apply to activities carried out under Part D of Title II)
   • Strategies for improving student academic achievement or substantially increasing the knowledge and teaching skills of teachers

◆ Are designed to give teachers of limited English proficient children, and other teachers and instructional staff, the knowledge and skills to provide instruction and appropriate language and academic support services to those children, including the appropriate use of curricula and assessments.

◆ To the extent appropriate, provide training for teachers and principals in the use of technology so that technology and technology applications are effectively used in the classroom to improve teaching and learning in the curricula and core academic subjects in which the teachers teach.

◆ As a whole, are regularly evaluated for their impact on increased teacher effectiveness and improved student academic achievement, with the findings of the evaluations used to improve the quality of professional development.

◆ Provide instruction in methods of teaching children with special needs.

◆ Include instruction in the use of data and assessments to inform and instruct classroom practice.

◆ Include instruction in ways that teachers, principals, pupil services personnel, and school administrators may work more effectively with parents.

2. May include activities that

◆ Involve the forming of partnerships with institutions of higher education to establish school-based teacher training programs that provide prospective teachers and beginning teachers with an opportunity to work under the guidance of experienced teachers and college faculty.

◆ Create programs to enable paraprofessionals (assisting teachers employed by a local educational agency receiving assistance under Part A of Title I) to obtain the education necessary for those paraprofessionals to become certified and licensed teachers.

◆ Provide follow-up training to teachers who have participated in activities described in subparagraph (A) or another clause of this subparagraph that is designed to ensure that the knowledge and skills learned by the teachers are implemented in the classroom [Title IX, Part A, Section 9101(34)].

Source: U.S. Department of Education (2002). *Improving Teacher Quality State Grants. Title II, Part A, Non-Regulatory Guidance.* http://www.ed.gov/offices/OESE/SIP/TitleIIguidance2002.doc.

Implementing school improvement—whether in the classroom by trying new strategies and procedures or schoolwide by modifying curriculum, ways in which school personnel interact with parents, or implementing new ways of doing things—requires a commitment to professional development. The commitment to professional development is needed because school improvement, broadly speaking, is about change—in practices, attitudes, beliefs, and the like.

What should professional development that supports school improvement look like? In the report, *Revisioning Professional Development: What Learner-centered Professional Development Looks Like* (National Partnership for Excellence and Accountability in Teaching, 1999a), the authors make several suggestions (see Figure 6.4).

Characteristics of Effective Professional Development

School improvement signals change, and one of the most important roles of the principal in supporting teachers' efforts at change is the facilitation of ongoing support. A comprehensive professional development program that prepares teachers for change and supports their learning needs during change must employ a variety of learning opportunities for teachers. Professional development is essential to any school improvement effort because *"students learn only from teachers who are themselves in the process of learning"* (McCall, 1997, p. 23, emphasis in the original). According to Abdal-Haqq (1996), effective professional development to ensure learning

- is ongoing;
- includes training, practice, and feedback; opportunities for individual reflection and group inquiry into practice; and coaching or other follow-up procedures;
- is school-based and embedded in teacher work;
- is collaborative, providing opportunities for teachers to interact with peers;
- focuses on student learning, which should, in part, guide assessment of its effectiveness;
- encourages and supports school-based and teacher initiatives;
- is rooted in the knowledge base for teaching;
- incorporates constructivist approaches to teaching and learning;
- recognizes teachers as professionals and adult learners;
- provides adequate time and follow-up support; and
- is accessible and inclusive.

Figure 6.4. Professional Development and School Improvement

- The content of professional development focuses on what students are to learn and how to address the different problems students may have in learning the material.

- Professional development should be based on analyses of the differences between (a) actual student performance and (b) goals and standards for student learning.

- Professional development should involve teachers in identifying what they need to learn and in developing the learning experiences in which they will be involved.

- Professional development should be primarily school-based and built into the day-to-day work of teaching.

- Most professional development should be organized around collaborative problem solving.

- Professional development should be continuous and ongoing, involving follow-up and support for further learning—including support from sources external to the school that can provide necessary resources and new perspectives.

- Professional development should incorporate evaluation of multiple sources of information on (a) outcomes for students and (b) the instruction and other processes involved in implementing lessons learned through professional development.

- Professional development should provide opportunities to understand the theory underlying the knowledge and skills being learned.

- Professional development should be connected to a comprehensive change process focused on improving student learning.

Source: National Partnership for Excellence and Accountability in Teaching (1999a, p. 3). *Revisioning Professional Development: What Learner-Centered Professional Development Looks Like.* http://www.nsdc.org/NPEAT213.pdf.

The ongoing nature of school improvement, including data collection and analysis along with issues related to implementation and refinement of strategies based on data analysis, points to several ideas about professional development. Professional development needs to be job-embedded, promote discussion, and supported through such methods as peer coaching, mentoring, and action research.

Job-Embedded Learning

Learning that is job-embedded "occurs as teachers and administrators engage in their daily work activities" (Wood & Killian, 1998, p. 52). It is unrealistic to expect teachers to implement strategies without such supports as peer coaching and mentoring so that teachers can learn in the setting of their classroom, as they are involved in the learning of their students. The real work of school improvement occurs in classrooms, and this is where dual learning occurs in that teachers should be learning because of implementing new strategies; however, given the hectic work-life of teachers, their learning often occurs far removed from their own classrooms.

Effective school improvement can be enhanced when teachers are encouraged to observe one another, discuss what occurs while they are teaching, and reflect openly in the presence of others who understand firsthand the complexities of the classroom.

There are four attributes of successful job-embedded learning:

1. It is relevant to the individual teacher.

2. Feedback is part of the process.

3. It facilitates the transfer of new skills into practice.

4. It supports reflection.

There are four essential conditions to ensure successful implementation of job-embedded professional development:

1. *Learning needs to be consistent with the principles of adult learning:* Learning goals are realistic; learning is relevant to the teacher, and concrete opportunities for practice of skills being learned are afforded.

2. *Trust in the process, in colleagues, and in the learner him/herself:* For learning to occur on the job, teachers must be able to trust the process (e.g., peer coaching, videotape analysis), their colleagues, and themselves. Teachers need to know that feedback will be constructive, not personal.

3. *Time within the regular school day needs to be made available for learning:* Traditionally, staff development takes place after hours, usually at

some remote site. Job-embedded learning requires time to be available within the context of the normal working day at the teacher's school site.

4. *Sufficient resources must be available to support learning:* Providing release time for teachers' professional development requires the creative use of human resources. In addition, outside facilitators are sometimes needed to assist teachers in learning new skills. Funding must be made available to meet these costs (Zepeda, 1999).

Peer Coaching

Peer coaching supports job-embedded learning in that teachers take the time during the day to observe one another teach. Parallel to the clinical model of instructional supervision, peer-coaching teams engage in pre-observation conferences, extended classroom observations, and post-observation conferences. Through peer coaching, teachers can assess implementation of school improvement strategies in the classroom by focusing on

- ◆ The skills teachers are implementing in practice
- ◆ The skills that teachers are struggling to implement
- ◆ What is working in practice—how and why
- ◆ The ongoing support and resources that teachers need
- ◆ Follow-up activities needed to support implementation

Regardless of whether peers engage in peer coaching or whether administrators employ the clinical model of classroom supervision, ongoing support is essential for teacher and student learning:

> *Most important,* teachers must be supported by self-assessment and reflection tools that help them assess fundamental beliefs and assumptions about learning, learners, and teaching....They must be guided by a process of reflection to identify those personal characteristics and/or practices that must change to improve motivation and achievement for each student. (McCombs, 1997, p. 12, emphasis in the original)

Differentiated and Developmental Supervisory Practices

The intents of supervision are primarily to promote professional growth and development. To promote professional growth and development, instructional supervision needs to be responsive to the needs of teachers across the career continuum, because the needs of teachers at the beginning, middle, and later stages of their careers are different. A teacher with less than three years experience would encounter different issues while implementing new strategies than a teacher with 15 or more years of experience. Effective principals know their teachers, and they know what their learning needs are. How do these principals know the learning needs of their teachers? They ask, they review the types of professional development activities their teachers have engaged in recently, they observe their teachers (both formal and informal observations), and they listen to teachers when they discuss instruction and student learning.

Principals actively seek out differentiated methods of working with teachers by examining the research base on such models as peer coaching, portfolio development, action research, and study groups. The scope of this book does not allow for an elaborate discussion of any of these models; however, these models can assist with the overall intent of school improvement—getting schools, their students, teachers, and parents to an improved state of learning.

Monitoring the School Improvement Plan

With school the improvement plan in operation, the attention of the school improvement team and principal shifts to monitoring the plan. Monitoring the plan occurs on several levels. First, a distinction is made—the plan is being evaluated based on its implementation, and the work toward meeting the goals is being assessed. We live in tough times for school improvement because the reality is that how students perform on tests is how teachers and administrators will be evaluated. This kind of thinking could breed mistrust of the efforts at school improvement. The principal will need to reconcile the approach while monitoring and assessing the school improvement plan.

Research shows that the more collaborative the culture, the higher the levels of trust among teachers and among teachers and administrators, and a focused vision on school improvement will yield results that are more favorable. School improvement is linked to change, and teachers are being asked to "put their instructional practices on the line" as a means to bolster student learning.

School improvement plans contain goals for improvement, and the areas targeted by the goals are the ones deemed in need of improvement. If data were used to find the gaps, the data serve as a baseline and act as a marker to the current situation. Examine the following target:

> By June 2003 the percentage of fourth-grade students scoring below standard in math problem solving will decrease by 15 percent.

With this target, it is obvious that a certain number of students at the fourth grade are performing and scoring below standard on math problem solving skills. This target is time-bound—there is a beginning point and ending point of measure. Monitoring cannot begin until the beginning point is identified.

Documenting Results

Just as data led to the development of the target, data must guide the school improvement team in analyzing progress toward meeting the end. The work of the team is to identify the types of data that will provide a formative (ongoing) view of how students are progressing toward the goal while simultaneously identifying what strategies are being used to fill the gap. The intent is to figure out what is working and more importantly, what is not working. Figure 6.5 illustrates this concept.

Figure 6.5. Framing the Assessment

Target	Data Used to Determine Gap	Strategies to Implement	Formative Assessments to Measure the Movement Toward Improvement	Final Assessments
By June 2003, the percentage of fourth-grade students scoring below standard in math problem solving will decrease by 15 percent.	♦ Grade 3 ♦ ITBSCOGAT			

By identifying this information, the team asks and answers several questions while broadly profiling the school improvement effort. The questions that people ask and the efforts teachers pursue to reach school improvement communicate priorities, and both the questions and the answers will guide ongoing school improvement efforts. These questions include

- ♦ What measures are to be used to chart progress toward the goal?
- ♦ When will data be collected and by whom?
- ♦ How often will data be collected?
- ♦ How will data be presented?

The school improvement team and the teachers of the fourth-grade students would eventually be able to

- Track progress for each student and for larger groups of students by teacher, class, section, or grade as a whole.

- Pull data on students who did not meet the mark and look for patterns across specific subscores.

- Speculate on either why or why not students made progress.

- Identify specific teaching strategies, curricular modifications, and staff development that is making a difference in student achievement.

- Possibly make cross-comparisons about several data sets.

- Raise questions about why the "data look the way it does" relative to findings.

Once data have been collected and analyzed, it is time to examine the strategies and the impact they are having on improvement. This is also the time to make mid-stream adjustments based on what has been learned.

According to *School Improvement Maryland* (n.d.), a professional learning community will focus on substantive issues and communicate the importance of those issues by employing the following process:

- Identify the criteria with which it will monitor the advancement toward its vision, the presence of its values, and the accomplishment of its goals.

- Systematically gather information on those criteria.

- Share data with the entire staff.

- Engage the entire staff in collective analysis of the information that is gathered.

- Develop new strategies for achieving its objectives more effectively.

- Carefully monitor the results of implementing those strategies. (http://www.mdk12.org/. ./data/progress/monitor_school.html.)

Chapter 5 examined data overload in relation to collecting data to find the gaps as a means to plan for school improvement. In this chapter, data overload is examined in relation to monitoring the school improvement plan and the areas targeted for improvement. Data overload is a distinct possibility, and that is why a school should be selective and prioritize its efforts at school improvement. It is easy to enumerate many goals, but the follow-up relative to monitoring and data collection will become unwieldy. The principal must remember that the members of the school improvement team, albeit leaders, are full-time teachers. Consider the possible data sources for tracking the process of teachers changing their practices to enhance math problem-solving skills at the fourth grade:

- Standardized tests
- Teacher-generated tests and quizzes
- Staff development
- The curriculum
- Teaching materials—books and other resource materials, including technology
- Remediation and enrichment opportunities

This list could continue, and this is why two or three targeted school improvement goals are more than enough to keep teachers focused on improvement. By examining data, the school will be able to define further the gaps that exist and to make subsequent plans based on the findings. It is through the examination of data that mid-course changes can be made if necessary. Later in the chapter, the implementation dip will be discussed. Perhaps the most helpful work of the principal is to shepherd the team through the process and to clear obstacles from teachers focusing on what they know how to do, and that is to assess learning and to develop the plan to forward improved teaching and learning based on data. The work of the principal involves the cognitive preparation for the meetings, setting the tone of the meetings, and conducting the meetings as developed in the following case from the field.

Understanding Data—A Precursor to Reviewing Efforts and Modifying Goals, Objectives, and Strategies

One obstacle in the school improvement process is handling an inordinate amount of data; another obstacle is understanding data. Karen Yarbrough, principal of Sonny Carter Elementary School, and Kelly Nagle, former assistant principal, developed a coordinated staff development plan to help teachers work with data and in the process think of data as a way to

- Ensure decisions about instruction are made based on data.
- Monitor strategies being implemented.
- Track student progress.
- Access overall impact of instructional efforts on student learning.
- Rethink what works and what does not appear to be working in a fault-free manner.

Superintendent Sharon Patterson explains that the Carter case is a clear example of a principal serving as the instructional leader of the school. We look at school-based staff development as a skill necessary to achieve school improvement and to improve the technical competence of the staff. The following explains the process that Yarbrough developed to work with data in a way in which teachers could make sense of it all.

Data Analysis— A Case from the Field

Sonny Carter Elementary School
5910 Zebulon Road
Macon, GA 31210
Karen D. Yarbrough, Principal
Phone (478) 471–5440 (Phone)
(478) 757–5536 (Fax)
kyarbrough.Carter@bibb.k12.ga.us

Kelly Nagle,
former Assistant Principal

Sharon Patterson, Superintendent
Bibb County School District
Bibb County, GA

Sonny Carter Elementary School serves Pre-K through sixth graders in Bibb County, Georgia. During 2002–2003, Sonny Carter served approximately 530 students. The population during that school year was 55% white, 39% African American, and 6% other minorities. Twenty-seven percent of the students received free or reduced price lunch and 14% received special education services. Fifty-five percent of the 30 certified staff members had advanced degrees.

Involving Teachers in Data Collection and Analysis

Involving teachers in data and test score analysis has been a long-standing practice at Sonny Carter Elementary School. Karen Yarbrough and the teachers at Sonny Carter Elementary School have worked together since the school opened to plan instruction based on results of the Iowa Test of Basic Skills (ITBS), the Stanford Achievement Test Ninth Edition (SAT 9), the Georgia Writing Assessment, and, most recently, the Georgia Criterion Referenced Competency Test (GA CRCT). Each year teachers compile accountability information on each child in their classroom, which then becomes part of Yarbrough's records. The teachers track how long the students have been at Sonny Carter Elementary School and a variety of achievement information, including test scores. Crafted in 2002–2003, the accountability form (Figure 6.6) helps to develop a baseline profile for each student.

Figure 6.6. Sonny Carter Elementary School Accountability Information

Student's Name _____

Grade_____ Homeroom Teacher_____

Entered Carter School on _____ From _____

Promoted/Retained/Placed_____

Number of schools in which previously enrolled_____

Norm-referenced Testing Scores (Name of Test _____)

Subject	2002 NPR	2003 NPR	Gain/Loss	2002 NCE	2003 NCE	Gain/Loss
Reading Total						
Reading Advanced						
Language Total						
Math Total						

	BLT (Basic Literacy Test)		OR		Star Assessment Reading Level	
2001–2002	2002–2003	Gain/Loss		Fall 2002	Spring 2003	Gain/Loss

CRCT Test Scores

Subject	2002 Scaled Score	2003 Scaled Score	Gain/Loss
Reading			
Language Arts			
Math			

In School Testing: WIAT (Wechsler Individual Achievement Test)

Date Administered	Math	Reading	Spelling

Other Information

Classroom Performance/Grades					
Reading	English	Spelling	Math	Science	Social Studies

Note special services received: _____

Psychological on file:_____

Requesting Help from Within and Beyond the School

Marked improvement on the GA Fifth Grade Writing Assessment during the past three years demonstrated the need for the administration to work closely with teachers to make sure they had all of the information they needed about students, testing, and results. After analyzing the spring 2000 writing scores, teachers in all grade levels worked with a writing consultant from the Georgia Department of Education in a process called "Power Writing." After the spring 2001 scores were analyzed, as the teachers of Sonny Carter Elementary School saw growth in their students' writing, they retrained in "Power Writing" to ensure retention of knowledge of those instructional methods, and used a curriculum specialist from within Bibb County, Dr. Mae Sheftall, to work with teachers on the "Writer's Workshop."

Reviewing Efforts and Results of Achieving Goals

There was no teacher turnover in any of the upper grades (fourth, fifth, or sixth) during this time; the same teachers were looking at their students' scores and their teaching practices each year and making adjustments for success. Scores illustrated that this type of analysis was working (Figure 6.7).

**Figure 6.7. Sonny Carter Elementary School—
Georgia Fifth Grade Writing Assessment Results**

	Spring 2000	Spring 2001	Spring 2002
Emerging Writers	0.0%	0.0%	0.0%
Developing Writers	0.0%	0.0%	0.0%
Focusing Writers	8.5%	0.9%	0.0%
Experimenting Writers	48.5%	28.1%	12.7%
Engaging Writers	40.0%	51.8%	39.7%
Extending Writers	3.1%	19.3%	47.6%

During 2002–2003, Yarbrough was selected as a first cohort participant in the Georgia Leadership Institute for School Improvement, which is a School Improvement initiative for Georgia school leaders funded by the Bill and Melinda Gates Foundation. Participation in this program validated Yarbrough's belief that data analysis should be consistent and pervasive throughout the instructional program at Sonny Carter Elementary School. Based on this training, the success of the students, and the empowerment of the teachers from previous data analysis, Karen Yarbrough and Kelly Nagle then planned a program to assist teachers in understanding and analyzing CRCT data. Spring of 2002 was the first time all students in grades one through six were tested on the CRCT, so each grade level had test results with which to work. Teachers were accustomed to analyzing norm-referenced information from the ITBS and/or SAT 9. Because the CRCT is a criterion-referenced test, teachers needed information about how to read criterion-referenced scores and how to use that information to help plan instruction.

Providing Staff Development to Assist Teachers in Understanding the Results of Data

Yarbrough designed a yearlong staff development program for analyzing student achievement data. This plan provided for 10 hours of release time for teachers in each grade, levels one through six, spread out over four days in two- to three-hour increments during the year. Building-level staff development allotments were used to pay substitute teachers to cover classes, while teachers worked in small groups with Yarbrough and Nagle. With only the principal, assistant principal, and three to four teachers at the table at a time, they were able to talk about specific information, specific subdomains on the test, and specific children, and to ask questions and present ideas and solutions in a safe, nonthreatening environment. Given the small size of each group, teachers were able to collaborate and to plan what needed to be accomplished to work with students to meet their learning needs.

At the first session with each grade level, teachers received copies of their class roster reports, and they spent time talking about what information the reports actually provided and how to read them. The group discussed scaled scores, percentages versus percentiles, and the difference between meeting and exceeding expectations. As a group, members also devised a color-coded legend for teachers to use in coding their class roster score summaries to spot trends and patterns, both for individual children and whole classes. Teachers color-coded the results to reflect children who were brand new to the building, who received free or reduced lunch, or who were *cusp* kids—students who scored within 5 points either way of the passing score. By looking at the performance of individual children and the class performance by subdomain, teachers gained an understanding of their areas of strength and weakness, as well as those of their students.

Assessing What Works

Teachers received both the scores of the children they taught the previous year to assess their own instructional effectiveness and the scores of the children they were currently teaching to assess their strengths and weaknesses to develop a more individualized instructional program. Teachers then completed the CRCT Class Roster Summary (Figure 6.8, p. 147) and determined Preliminary Strengths (Figure 6.9, p. 148) and Preliminary Areas for Improvement (Figure 6.10, p. 149) based on these color-coded scores.

Teachers took this information and were given time to digest it; they worked together in grade-level meetings for the four to six weeks following the initial session and also looked at their scores individually. When the groups came back together for the second and third sessions, teachers brought their coded scores and the results of their analyses. Yarbrough, Nagle, and the teachers talked through the questions that were identified as areas of need, and they created summaries for each teacher and each grade level. Teachers of each grade level summarized their individual analyses by completing the Summary Report of All Student Populations (Figure 6.11, p. 150) and made Data Summary Statements (Figure 6.12, p. 151). These tables and forms were adapted from information provided to trainees during the Georgia Leadership Institute training.

Specifically in the area of math, Sonny Carter teachers were also working with a consultant during 2002–2003. The groups shared results with the consultant to devise plans for staff development training designed by grade level to address weaknesses cited in the data analysis by improving content preparation of teachers and meeting the instructional needs of each student. Weaknesses were identified specifically by objectives on the test.

(Text continues on page 152.)

Figure 6.8. Sonny Carter Elementary School
CRCT Class Roster Summary

Content Area: _____

Grade level: _____

Strengths: Subjects/Subdomains where percentage of students meeting or exceeding standards is high—80 percent or above. This means that 80 percent or more students are scoring at Performance Levels 2 and 3. *Tip: It may be quicker for you to scan the column for level for any groups that are 20 percent or less than to add levels 2 and 3.*

Subject/Subdomain	Percentage Meeting/Exceeding Standards Spring 2002

Preliminary Areas for Improvement: Subjects/Subdomains where percentage of students Not Meeting Standards is relatively high—35 percent or above. This means that 35 percent or more of the students are scoring at Performance Level 1.

Subject/Subdomain	Percentage Not Meeting/Exceeding Standards Spring 2002

Figure 6.9. Sonny Carter Elementary School
CRCT Data Analysis—Preliminary Strengths

Grade level: _____

Preliminary Strengths: Areas where percentage of students meeting or exceeding standards and where year-to-year gains appear relatively high.			
Content Area	*Subgroup*	*Meeting/Exceeding in Current Year*	*Gain from Previous Year*
Reading			
English/Language Arts			
Mathematics			
Social Studies			
Science			

**Figure 6.10. Sonny Carter Elementary School
CRCT Data Analysis—Preliminary Areas for Improvement**

Grade level: _____

Homeroom teacher: _____

Preliminary Areas for Improvement: Areas where percentage of students not meeting standards appears high and where year-to-year gains appear relatively low.

Content Area	Subgroup	Not Meeting Standards in Current Year	Change from Previous Year
Reading			
English/Language Arts			
Mathematics			
Social Studies			
Science			

Figure 6.11. Sonny Carter Elementary School
CRCT Summary Report of All Student Populations

Content Area: _____

Grade level: _____

Strengths: Groups where percentage of students meeting or exceeding standards is high—80 percent or above. This means that 80 percent or more students are scoring at Performance Levels 2 and 3. Tip: It may be quicker for you to scan the column for level for any groups that are 20 percent or less than to add Levels 2 and 3.	
Subgroup	*Percentage Meeting/Exceeding Standards Spring 2002*

Preliminary Areas for Improvement: Groups where percentage of students not meeting standards is relatively high—35 percent or above. This means that 35 percent or more of the students are scoring at Performance Level 1.	
Subgroup	*Percentage Not Meeting/Exceeding Standards Spring 2002*

Figure 6.12. Sonny Carter Elementary School
CRCT Data Summary Statements

Content area: _____

Grade level: _____

Prepare a statement summarizing your results from the analysis of the CRCT data. Complete a summary for each subject area, and include general information about overall performance in the subject area for your grade level. Include relative strengths among the disaggregated student groups and areas that are in greatest need of additional instructional support.

_____

_____

_____

_____

_____

_____

_____

_____

_____

_____

_____

_____

_____

_____

_____

_____

_____

_____

_____

_____

_____

_____

Teachers also used their analysis of individual student results to make accommodations in Student Support Team plans and to implement strategies in their classrooms to remediate deficiencies. They wrote goals for Annual Improvement based on test subdomains and subpopulations. Teachers conferenced with individual children to discuss strengths and weaknesses and to give the children ownership in the process. Teachers used the Item Response Analysis reports to devise daily instructional focus lessons. These lessons were designed to address instructional weaknesses revealed through analysis of students' responses on specific items on the CRCT. During this analysis, teachers used released test items to analyze student responses to determine the reason for errors. Errors were ranked in order of need by the percentage of students who missed the question and the weight of the subject domain. Instructional focus calendars and a timeline were developed to address these areas of need through a "test blitz" that was implemented for six weeks prior to the testing. During this blitz, 10-minute instructional focus lessons were developed and taught to remediate identified deficiencies. Mini-assessments consisting of no more than four to five questions were prepared and administered intermittently to check student understanding of the content delivered during the instructional focus lessons. The results of these assessments enabled teachers to prescribe appropriate remedial or enrichment activities.

The work the teachers did with these scores is kept on file with Yarbrough, and the data serve as a working plan from which to design instruction, create school improvement and staff development plans, and follow the progress of students and teachers (Figure 6.13).

Sustaining the Momentum for School Improvement

Bringing about school improvement is tiring work for teachers, students, parents, and administrators. The challenge for the principal is to keep the momentum going by keeping the efforts of the community focused on the importance and value of school improvement efforts.

Understanding Change

Why is school improvement so daunting? First, during school improvement (no matter how small or big), teachers, administrators, students, and parents are being asked to think and do things differently. Second, school improvement signals multiple changes that are interrelated, and these multiple changes require monitoring several items at a time. Third, change is fast-paced, but sometimes achieving the desired results is slow-paced.

Figure 6.13. Sonny Carter Elementary School
CRCT Student Assessment Annual Improvement Goals

Teacher's Name (if applicable): _____

Grade Level: _____

Subject/ Subdomain	Population Targeted for Improvement (Example: Females in Level 1)	Percentage in 2002	Projected Percentage in 2003	Action Steps to Be Taken

Throughout the process of school improvement, teachers will be modifying goals and strategies needed to reach improvement. Teachers will be involved in examining practices, examining data as a gauge of hitting or missing the mark, and rethinking what works and what does not seem to be working. For the principal, this means sustaining the momentum by cheering and encouraging teachers, their efforts, and the efforts of students—even if results are less than expected.

To sustain the momentum for school improvement, the principal must understand change and risk. The reader is encouraged to examine Chapter 2 for the discussion on the norms, values, and beliefs because these factors shape the school and any subsequent movement toward school improvement. The school's culture and climate will affect change. It is the principal's role to set forth the conditions necessary for teachers to implement change, because change is integral to school improvement processes. "School cultures are incredibly resistant to change. This is precisely why school improvement—from within or from without—is usually so futile," are the words of Barth (2001b, p. 8) who despite the anguish involved in change, believes that schools can rise to the occasion and make the changes necessary to improve learning and leading. Figure 6.14 provides a broad overview of assumptions about change, leadership, and school improvement.

Facing Implementation Dips

Once data are available, principals and teachers need to take stock of the reality of the efforts while monitoring the school improvement plan and its many goals and objectives. The key question is, *Are we getting the desired results based on the strategies or modifications we are implementing?* Teachers will not want to answer this question unless there is a norm of safety to engage in fault-free problem posing and solving. Principals can avoid falling into the trap of finger pointing by taking a stance of *no blame* and a resolve to provide (1) time for discussion, (2) time for further exploration, and (3) more time to let the modification to be tested. Time is needed because often with implementation comes what is referred to as an *implementation dip.* Fullan (2001) suggests in his book, *Leading in a Culture of Change,* people need to "appreciate the implementation dip" (p. 34).

An implementation dip occurs, in part, because people are trying new techniques and they are refining their practices. The saying, "We are building the plane while flying it," comes to mind when thinking about the implementation dip and incorporating new strategies to target areas in need of improvement. A knee-jerk reaction is to discontinue the new practice because immediate results are not being realized.

Figure 6.14. Assumptions About
Change Related to Leadership

Assumptions about Change (CBAM) (Hord, Rutherford, Huling-Austin, & Hall, (1987))	Leadership Needed by the Principal (Calabrese (2002))	Leadership Translated to Action
◆ Change is a process, not an event. ◆ Change is accomplished by individuals. ◆ Change is a highly personal experience. ◆ Change involves developmental growth. ◆ Change is best understood in operational terms. ◆ The focus of facilitation should be on individuals, and the context. (pp. 5–6)	◆ Leaders meet the needs of their constituents ◆ Leaders create a sense of personal urgency for change among members of the organization. ◆ Leaders sustain change by learning to manage the pace of change. ◆ Effective change leaders construct a climate that encourages organizational members to gain a personal understanding of their status and weigh that understanding against the potential for improvement. ◆ The leader constructs a psychologically safe environment in which members are free to question their beliefs and values without the risk of threat or embarrassment. (pp. 11–15)	◆ Involving teachers as leaders; ◆ Supporting improvement through supervision and evaluation procedures that are responsive to teacher needs; ◆ Creating and maintaining an environment conducive to innovation and risk-taking; ◆ Providing ongoing staff development to support teacher and administrative learning; ◆ Facilitating open and honest communication about innovations; and, ◆ Securing necessary resources for supporting change.

Sources: Calabrese (2002); Hord, Rutherford, Huling-Austin, & Hall (1987).

The implementation dip is especially important to consider since school improvement plans typically span more than one year and sometimes to see the fruition of results in increased student learning, several iterations of an innovation are needed. Given the long-term and ongoing nature of school improvement, the school needs to ready for a long-term view of school improvement using data as a guide.

With an open eye to possible implementation dips, the principal can help "hold the fort" if teachers and community members begin to push for the abandonment of a school improvement strategy. The principal can work with the school improvement team to

1. Collect data—use baseline data as the beginning point to examine all future data collected.

2. Engage stakeholders in the discussion of implementation strategies—perhaps mid-course corrections need to be made. Encourage the examination of artifacts (lesson plans, results of classroom assessments—portfolios, quizzes, student papers.

3. Use action research strategies as a follow-up to implementation.

4. Work with other schools (in and outside of the system) to see what is working and why or why not.

Much can be learned about the implementation of a strategy by careful analysis of results. It is the examination of individual and then collective practices and results over time that will lead the school in determining the future direction of particular school improvement strategies.

The principal needs to help teachers sift through their disappointment and work toward refining practice; the principal needs to assure teachers they are on the right track and provide additional resources such as opportunities to engage in peer coaching and off-site visitations to buildings where similar strategies are being used. Teachers need time to exchange ideas and to give feedback to one another. It is through the exchange of ideas and perspectives that new approaches will emerge.

Exploring What is Blocking Progress Toward Meeting Goals

Fullan (2001) also offers that leaders need to "redefine resistance" (p. 34). People naturally resist change, but sometimes good ideas can emerge from the voices of those who are resisting change. The principal might glean important ideas from those who are publicly objecting to modification in practice. Perhaps the resisters are doing so because they have an alternate point of view that can offer a better or equally sound way of approaching a solution to a problem of practice. However, not all resisters are vocal. The principal is wise to keep lines of communication open, speaking frequently with all teachers, offering assistance, showing support, and respecting the expertise that teachers bring through their years of experience.

There can be other obstacles to meeting targets beside resistance to change. The principal might consider the following reasons:

♦ *The need to learn new skills*: A comprehensive program of staff development can assist teachers in learning new skills. Follow-up assistance, including additional learning opportunities, classroom observations by the principal or a peer coach, mentoring, study groups, and action research pairs, is a proactive way to keep the momentum for change in the forefront.

♦ *Outdated resources*: Implementing school improvement might necessitate rethinking how resources are allocated. While planning, implementing, and monitoring school improvement efforts, the principal should ask, what materials, staff development, and resources will be needed to carry out the plan? There might be a need to purchase supplementary learning materials for both students and teachers or to alter the master schedule to allot time for teachers to meet or extend certain class periods. Other resources could include reaching out to the central office or other constituents such as parents. Local universities can also provide resources such as faculty expertise. Given tight budgets, principals might need to become entrepreneurial and seek external funding through grants or enter into partnerships with local business and community members.

♦ *Holdouts*: Some people just will not get with the program; they are the holdouts. The principal will need to try myriad approaches to working with the holdouts—from encouragement to purposefully applying tension. The principal who purposefully monitors progress will discover who the holdouts are and, in the final analysis, will need to confront the people who are making less than desirable efforts. The approach to confronting should be guided by the heart—what is in the best interest of the person and the best interest of students, the benefactors of school improvement efforts. Here are a few tips:

♦ Track indicators and privately share these indicators with the teacher.

♦ Have suggestions ready to offer—every attempt should be made to help the holdout get on the same proverbial page of the school improvement effort.

♦ Enlist the support of others to provide assistance, such as another member of the administrative team, a central office administrator, or lead teacher.

In the final analysis, the principal might have to make a personnel decision such as placing the holdout on a plan of improvement, but such a strategy should be the absolute last route, in that the last thing the principal wants to do is create a sense of fear in other members of the faculty.

Shining the Light

Given the nature of school improvement and the commitment it takes to sustain the journey, the principal needs to "cheer the troops" for both small and big accomplishments. Clemmer (n.d.) suggests, "Effective leaders break the endless improvement journey into a series of short exciting trips. A key element of that is celebrating and savoring successes. It's how effective improvement leaders reenergize everyone to strive for the next goal." He gives two strategies:

♦ Show appreciation for good tries, pilots, and mistakes that advance organization learning, especially if that experience is shared openly and widely for all to benefit from and build on.

♦ As with communications, use every recognition channel you can— public and private, oral and written—to reinforce and support success, accomplishments, and progress. http://www.clemmer.net/excerpts/pp_recognition.shtml.

Suggested Readings

Baker, P. J. (1997). Building better schools: How to initiate, sustain and celebrate school improvement. *Planning & Changing, 28*(3), 130–138.

Bryk, A. S., & Schneider, B. (2002). *Trust in schools: A core resource for improvement.* New York: Russell Sage.

Corson, D. J. School improvement by design. Area Education Agency 7, Cedar Falls, Iowa at http://edservices.aea7.k12.ia.us/sibd/plans/index.html.

Fullan, M. (2001). *Leading in a culture of change.* San Francisco: Jossey-Bass.

Harris, A. (2002). *School improvement: What's in it for schools?* London: Routledge-Falmer.

Harris, A. (2000). What works in school improvement? Lessons from the field and future directions. *Educational Research, 42*(1), 1–11.

Joyce, B. R., & Showers, B. (2002). *Student achievement through staff development: fundamentals of school renewal* (3rd ed.). Alexandria, VA: Association for Supervision and Curriculum Development.

School Improvement in Maryland at http://www.mdk12.org/process/index.html.

References

Abdal-Haqq, I. (1996). *Making time for teacher professional development.* Washington, DC: ERIC Clearinghouse on Teaching and Teacher Education. (ERIC Document Reproduction Service No. ED400259).

Baker, P. J. (1997). Building better schools: How to initiate, sustain and celebrate school improvement. *Planning & Changing: A Journal for School Administrators, 28*(3), 130–138.

Baloche, L. A. (1998). *The cooperative classroom: Empowering learning.* Upper Saddle River, NJ: Prentice Hall.

Barth, R. S. (1990). Improving schools from within: Teachers, parents, and principals can make a difference. San Francisco: Jossey-Bass.

Barth, R. S. (2001a). Teacher leader. *Phi Delta Kappan 82*(6), 443–449.

Barth, R. S. (2001b). *Learning by heart.* San Francisco: Jossey-Bass.

Beck, L. G. (1992). Meeting the challenge of the future: The place of a caring ethic in educational administration. *American Journal of Education, 100*(4), 454–496.

Bennett, A. (2002). *Critical issue: Guiding principals—Addressing accountability challenges.* Retrieved July 27, 2003, from North Central Regional Educational Laboratory Web site: http://www.ncrel.org/sdrs/areas/issues/educatrs/leadrshp/le600.htm.

Bernauer, J. (2002). Five keys to unlock continuous improvement. *Kappa Delta Pi Record, 38*(2), 89–92.

Bernhardt, V. L. (2002). The school portfolio toolkit: A planning, implementation, and evaluation guide for continuous school improvement. Larchmont, NY: Eye on Education.

Bower, M. (1966). The will to manage. Corporate success through programmed management. New York: McGraw-Hill.

Bryk, A. S., & Schneider, B. (2002). *Trust in schools: A core resource for improvement.* New York: Russell Sage.

Calabrese, R. L. (2002). *The leadership assignment: Creating change.* Boston: Allyn and Bacon.

Calabrese, R. L., Short, G., & Zepeda, S. J. (1996). *Hands-on leadership tools for principals.* Larchmont, NY: Eye on Education.

Calabrese, R. L., & Zepeda, S. J. (1997). *The reflective supervisor.* Larchmont, NY: Eye on Education.

Chance, P. L., & Chance, E. W. (2002). Introduction to educational leadership and organizational behavior: Theory into practice. Larchmont, NY: Eye on Education.

Chapman, C. (2003). Building the leadership capacity for school improvement: A case study. In A. Harris, C. Day, D. Hopkins, M. Hadfield, A. Hargreaves, & C. Chapman (Eds.), *Effective leadership for school improvement* (pp. 137–153). London: RoutledgeFalmer.

Chenoweth, T. G., & Everhart, R. B. (2002). *Navigating comprehensive school change: A guide for the perplexed.* Larchmont, NY: Eye on Education.

Choo, C. W. (2001). Environmental scanning as information seeking and organizational learning. Information Research, 7(1). Retrieved July 27, 2003, from http://www.informationr.net/ir/7–1/paper112.html.

Christenson, M., Eldredge, F., Ibom, K., Johnston, M., & Thomas, M. (1996). Collaboration in support of change. *Theory into Practice, 35*(3), 187–195.

Clark, R. E., & Estes, F. (2002). Turning research into results: A guide to selecting the right performance solutions. Atlanta, GA: CEP Press.

Clemmer, J. (n.d.). *Pathways and pitfalls to giving personal recognition and appreciation.* Retrieved September 19, 2003, from http://www.clemmer.net/excerpts/pp_recognition.shtml.

Colorado State Department of Education (1999). *The SILC school improvement planning process: The SILC road.* Denver, CO: Colorado Department of Education. Retrieved November 3, 2003, from http://www.cde.state.co.us/cdesped/download/pdf/silc-School%20Improvement.pdf.

Comer, J. P. (2001). Schools that develop children. *The American Prospect, 12*(7). Retrieved May 9, 2003, from http://www.prospect.org/print/V12/7/comer-j.html.

Cook, T. D., Hunt, H. D., & Murphy, R. F. (1998) *Comer's school development program in Chicago: A theory-based evaluation.* Retrieved March 10, 2003, from Institute for Policy Research. Northwestern University Web site: http://www.northwestern.edu/ipr/publications/comer.pdf.

Cooley, V., & Shen, J. (2003). School accountability and professional job responsibilities: A perspective from secondary principals. *NASSP Bulletin 87*(634), 10–25.

Corson, D. J. (2000). *Desired state chart.* Retrieved December 25, 2002, from http://edservices.aea7.k12.ia.us/sibd/direction/desiredstate.html.

Corson, D. J. (2002). *Data sources in schools.* Retrieved December 7, 2002, from http://edservices.aea7.k12.ia.us/sibd/data/datasources.html.

Cromwell, S. (2002). Is your school's culture toxic or positive? *Education World.* Retrieved December 5, 2002, from http://www.education-world.com/a_admin/admin275.shtml.

Darling-Hammond, L. (1997). *Doing what matters most: Investing in quality teaching*. Retrieved July 25, 2003, from National Commission on Teaching and America's Future Web site: http://www.nctaf.org/publications/DoingWhatMattersMost.pdf.

Deal, T. E., & Peterson, K. D. (1999). *Shaping school culture: The heart of leadership*. San Francisco: Jossey-Bass.

Dimmock, C. (2002). School design: A classificatory framework for the 21st century approach to school improvement. *School Effectiveness and School Improvement, 13*(2), 137–162.

Dyer, W. G. (1995). *Team building: Current issues and new alternatives* (3rd ed.). Reading, MA: Addison-Wesley.

Eastwood, K. W., & Tallerico, M. (1990). School improvement planning teams: Lessons from practice. *Planning & Changing: A Journal for School Administrators, 21*(1), 3–12.

Education Quality and Accountability Office (2000). *Ontario Report and Guide on School Improvement Planning: 1999–2000*. Retrieved July 27, 2003, from http://www.eqao.com/eqao/home_page/pdf_e/00/00P056e.pdf.

Elementary and Secondary Education Act (ESEA) of 1965, Pub. L. No. 89–10, 79 stat. 27.

Fielder, D. J. (2003). *Achievement now! How to assure no child is left behind*. Larchmont, NY: Eye on Education.

Fink, D. (1999). Deadwood didn't kill itself: A pathology of failing schools. *Educational Management & Administration, 27*(2), 131–141.

Fiore, D. J. (2001). Creating connections for better schools: How leaders enhance school culture. Larchmont, NY: Eye on Education.

Fitzpatrick, K. A. (1997). *School improvement: Focusing on student performance*. Schaumburg, IL: National Study of School Evaluation.

Fullan, M. (1997). *What's worth fighting for in the principalship? Strategies for taking charge in the school principalship* (2nd ed.). Mississagua, ON: Ontario Public School Teachers' Federation.

Fullan, M. (2001). *Leading in a culture of change*. San Francisco: Jossey-Bass.

Fullan, M. (2002). The change leader. *Educational Leadership, 59*(8), 16–20.

Freiberg, J. (1998). Measuring school culture. *Educational Leadership, 56*(1), 22–26.

Frost, D., & Durrant, J. (2002). Teachers as leaders: Exploring the impact of teacher-led development work. *School Leadership and Management, 22*(2), 143–161.

Gandal, M., & McGiffert, L. (2003). The power of testing. *Educational Leadership, 60*(5), 39–42.

Goodlad, J. (1984). *A place called school: Prospects for the future*. New York: McGraw-Hill.

Government of Newfoundland and Labrador, Department of Education and Student Support Services. (1995). *Positive school climate*. Retrieved November 24, 2002, from http://www.edu.gov.nf.ca/discipline/pos_schl_clim.htm.

Hallinger, P., Bickman, L., & Davis, K. (1996). School context, principal leadership, and student reading achievement. *The Elementary School Journal, 96*(5), 527–549.

Hallinger, P., & Heck, R. H. (1998). Exploring the principal's contribution to school effectiveness: 1980–1995. *School Effectiveness and School Improvement 9*(2), 157–191.

Halpin, A., & Croft, D. (1963). *The organizational climate of schools*. Chicago: University of Chicago Press.

Hammonds, B., & Morris, W. (n.d.). *School as a community: How good is your teamwork?* Retrieved October 22, 2002, from Leading-learning.co.nz. Web site: http://www.leading-learning.co.nz/school-vision/teamwork-survey.html.

Hammonds, B., & Morris, W. (n.d.). *Quality learning: Eleven factors for effective schools*. Retrieved July 29, 2003 from http://www.leading-learning.co.nz/school-vision/eleven-factors.html.

Hammonds, B., & Morris, W. (n.d.). *Quality learning: Six factors contributing to improving schools*. Retrieved September 1, 2003, from http://www.leading-learning.co.nz/school-vision/six-factors.html.

Hargreaves, A. (1997). Cultures of teaching and educational change. In M. Fullan (Ed.), *The challenge of school change* (pp. 57–84). Arlington Heights, IL: Skylight Training and Publishing.

Harris, A. (2000). What works in school improvement? Lessons from the field and future directions. *Educational Research, 42*(1), 1–11.

Harris, A. (2002). *School improvement: What's in it for schools?* London: Routledge-Falmer.

Haydn, T. (2001). From a very peculiar department to a very successful school: Transference issues arising out of a study of an improving school. *School Leadership and Management, 21*(4), 415–439.

Hopkins, D., & Reynolds, D. (2001). The past, present, and future of school improvement: Towards a third age. *British Educational Research Journal, 27*(4), 459–475.

Hord, S. M., Rutherford, W. L., Huling-Austin, L., & Hall, G. E. (1987). *Taking charge of change*. Alexandria, VA: Association for Supervision and Curriculum Development.

Illinois State Board of Education (1999). A guide to an integrated school improvement planning framework: An opportunity for Illinois schools to integrate planning resources for continuous school improvement. Springfield, IL: Illinois State Board of Education. (Eric Documentation Reproduction Service No. 444260).

Indiana Department of Education. (2002). *Suggested approaches to school improvement planning.* Retrieved January 9, 2003, from http://doe.state.in.us/pba/suppb.html.

Indiana Department of Education—Division of Accountability (2003). *Suggested approaches to school improvement planning.* Retrieved August 3, 2003, from http://ideanet.doe.state.in.us/accreditation/suppb.html.

Joyce, B. R., & Showers, B. (2002). *Student achievement through staff development: Fundamentals of school renewal* (3rd ed.). Alexandria, VA: Association for Supervision and Curriculum Development.

Katzenbach, J. R., & Smith, D. K. (1993). *The wisdom of teams: Creating the high performance organization.* Boston: Harvard Business School Press.

Kofman, F., & Senge, P. (1993). Communities of commitments: The heart of learning organizations. *Organizational Dynamics, 22*(2), 5–23.

Komives, S. R. (1994). New approaches to leadership. In J. Fried (Ed.), *Different voices: Gender and perspective in student affairs administration* (pp. 46–61). Washington, DC: National Association of Student Personnel Administrators.

Kruse, S., & Louis, K. S. (1995). Teacher teaming—Opportunities and dilemmas. *Brief to Principals, 11,* 1–6. Madison, WI: Center on Organization and Restructuring of Schools, Wisconsin Center for Education Research, School of Education, University of Wisconsin-Madison.

Kruse, S., Louis, K. S., & Bryk, A. (1994). Building professional community in schools. *Issues in Restructuring Schools, 6,* 3–6. Madison, WI: Center on Organization and Restructuring of Schools, Wisconsin Center for Education Research, School of Education, University of Wisconsin-Madison.

Lambert, L. (1995). Toward a theory of constructivist leadership. In L. Lambert, D. Walker, D. P. Zimmerman, J. E. Cooper, M. D. Lambert, M. E. Gardner, & P. J. Slack (Eds.), *The constructivist leader* (pp. 28–51). New York: Teachers College Press.

Lambert, L. (2003). *Leadership capacity for lasting school improvement.* Alexandria, VA: Association for Supervision and Curriculum Development.

Lane, B. A. (1992). Cultural leaders in effective schools: The builders and brokers of excellence. *NASSP Bulletin 76*(541), 85–96.

Learning Center. *Meeting Check List From High Performance Teamwork and Quality Training Courses (2002).* Retrieved October 5, 2002, from http://www.learningcenter.net/ library/meeting.shtml.

Lefrancois, G. R. (1982). Psychology for teaching: A bear always usually sometimes rarely faces the front (4th ed.). Belmont, CA: Wadsworth.

Leithwood, K. (1992). The move toward transformational leadership. *Educational Leadership 49*(5), 8–12.

Leonard, L. J. (2002). Schools as professional communities: Addressing the collaborative challenge. *International Electronic Journal for Leadership in Learning, 6*(17). Retrieved September 9, 2002, from http://www.ucalgary.ca/~iejll/

Lieberman, A., & Miller, L. (1999). *Teachers—transforming their world and their work.* New York: Teachers College Press.

Lunenburg, F. C. (1995). *The principalship: Concepts and applications.* Englewood Cliffs, NJ: Merrill.

Maslow, A. H. (1987). *Motivation and personality* (Rev. ed.). New York: Harper & Row.

McCall, J. R. (1997). *The principal as steward.* Larchmont, NY: Eye on Education.

McCombs, B.L. (1997). Self-assessment and reflection: Tools for promoting teacher changes toward learner-centered practices. *NASSP Bulletin, 81*(587), 1–14.

McGuire, K. (2001). Do you have what it takes to be an effective school leader? *Curriculum Review, 41*(4), 14–16.

McInerney, W. D., & Leach, J. A. (1992). School improvement planning: evidence of impact. *Planning & Changing: A Journal for School Administrators, 23*(1), 15–28.

McTighe, J., & Thomas, R. S. (2003). Backward design for forward action. *Educational Leadership, 60*(5), 52–55.

Mendez-Morse, S. (1992). *Leadership characteristics that facilitate change.* Austin, TX: Southwest Educational Development Laboratory.

Mintrop, H., & MacLellan, A. M. (2002). School improvement plans in elementary and middle schools on probation. *The Elementary School Journal, 102*(4), 275–300.

Murphy, J., & Louis, K. S. (1994). *Reshaping the principal.* Thousand Oaks, CA: Corwin Press.

National Association of Elementary School Principals. (2001). *Leading learning communities: Standards for what principals should know and be able to do.* Alexandria, VA: Author.

National Commission on Excellence in Education (1983). *A nation at risk: The imperative for educational reform. A report to the nation and the secretary of education.* Washington, DC: United States Department of Education.

National Commission on Teaching and America's Future (1996). *What matters most: Teaching for America's future.* New York: Author.

National Partnership for Excellence and Accountability in Teaching (1999a). *Revisioning Professional Development: What Learner-Centered Professional Devel-*

opment Looks Like. Retrieved March 10, 2003, from http://www.nsdc.org/NPEAT213.pdf.

National Partnership for Excellence and Accountability in Teaching (1999b). A Report of the National Partnership for Excellence and Accountability in Teaching. What learner-centered professional development looks like: Revisioning professional development. Retrieved April 5, 2003, from http://www.nsdc.org/NPEAT213.pdf.

National School Boards Foundation (n.d.). *Ten characteristics of well-functioning teams.* Retrieved November 10, 2002, from http://www.nsba.org/sbot/toolkit/LeadTeams.html.

No Child Left Behind (2003). *No Child Left Behind: A Parents Guide.* Retrieved July 21, 2003, http://www.nclb.org/next/parentsguide.html.

North Carolina State Department of Public Instruction (1999). *Planning for school improvement. NC HELPS: North Carolina helping education in low-performing schools.* Raleigh, NC: Author. (Eric Documentation Reproduction Service No. 439525).

North Central Regional Educational Laboratory (NCREL) (2003) *Learning Indicators.* Retrieved September 7, 2003, from http://www.ncrel.org/sdrs/ areas/issues/content/cntareas/math/ma21indi.htm.

Oxley, D. (1997). Theory and practice of school communities. *Educational Administration Quarterly, 33*(5), 624–644.

Peters, T., & Waterman, R. H. (1982). *In search of excellence.* New York: Harper & Row.

Peterson, K. D. (1999). Time use flows from school culture. *Journal of Staff Development, 20*(2), 16–19.

Peterson, K. D. (2002). Positive or negative? *Journal of Staff Development, 23*(3), 10–15.

Popham, W. J. (2001). *The truth about testing: An educator's call to action.* Alexandria, VA: Association for Supervision and Curriculum Development.

Robbins, P. & Alvy, H. B. (1995). *The principal's companion: Strategies and hints to make the job easier.* Thousand Oaks, CA: Corwin Press.

Rouda, R. H., & Kusy, M. E., Jr. (1995). *Needs assessment: The first step.* Retrieved July 28, 2003, from http://www.alumni.caltech.edu/~rouda/T2_NA.html.

Rudalevige, A. The politics of No Child Left Behind. *Education Next, A Journal of Opinion and Research, 3*(4), 63–69.

Sackney, L. (1988). *Enhancing school learning climate: Theory, research and practice. SSTA Research Report #180.* Retrieved November 10, 2002, from Saskatchewan School Trustees Association Research Centre Web site: http://www.ssta.sk.ca/research/school_improvement/180.htm.

Saphier, J., & King, M. (1985). Good seeds grow in strong cultures. *Educational Leadership, 42*(6), 67–74.

Schein, E. H. (1992). *Organizational Culture and Leadership* (2nd ed.). San Francisco: Jossey-Bass.

Schein, E. H. (1996). Culture: The missing concept in organization studies. *Administrative Science Quarterly, 41*(2), 229–240.

Schmoker, M., & Marzano, R. (1999). Realizing the promise of standards-based education. *Educational Leadership, 56*(6), 17–21.

School Improvement in Maryland (n.d.). Implementing the plan; Choosing strategies; both from *School Improvement in Maryland.* Retrieved September 1, 2003, from http://www.mdk12.org/process/10steps/7/index.html and http://www.mdk12.org/process/10steps/6/index.html.

Seashore-Louis, K., Toole, J., & Hargreaves, A. (1999). Rethinking school improvement. In J. Murphy and K. Seashore-Louis (Eds.), *Handbook of research on educational administration* (pp. 251–276). San Francisco: Jossey-Bass.

Seikaly, L. H. (2002). *Principal's role in creating a vision,* from *School Improvement in Maryland (MDK12).* Retrieved November 16, 2002, from http://www.mdk12.org/process/leading/principals_role.html.

Sergiovanni, T. J. (1995). *Leadership for the schoolhouse.* San Francisco: Jossey-Bass.

Short, R., & Greer, J. (1997). *Leadership for Empowered Schools.* Columbus, OH: Merrill.

Silva, D. Y., Gimbert, B., & Nolan, J. (2000). Sliding the doors: Locking and unlocking possibilities for teacher leadership. *Teachers College Record, 4*(102), 779–804.

Stanton, M. J. (1999). *Schools that teach: A blueprint for the millennium (updating school building space).* Retrieved November 21, 2002, from http://www.findarticles.com/ cf_dls/m1272/2650_128/55149350/p1/article.jhtml?term.

Sterline, M. (1998). Building a community week by week. *Educational Leadership, 56*(1), 65–68.

Stolp, S., & Smith, S. C. (1995). *Transforming school culture: Stories, symbols, values, and the leader's role.* Eugene, OR: ERIC Clearinghouse on Educational Management, University of Oregon.

Stone, S. J. (1995). Teaching strategies: Empowering teachers, empowering children. *Childhood Education 71*(5), 294–295.

Swist, J. (n.d.). *Conducting a training needs assessment.* Retrieved July 27, 2003, from http://www.amxi.com/amx_mi30.htm.

Tanner, C. T. (2002). *The school's learning environment.* Retrieved October 31, 2003, from School Design and Planning Laboratory at the University of Georgia Web site: http://www.coe.uga.edu/sdpl/sdpl.html.

The Teal Trust (2002) *Team process.* Retrieved November 2, 2002, from http://www.teal.org.uk/et/teampro.htm.

Thompson, D. C. (1992). School improvement and student outcomes: A resource perspective. *Planning & Changing: A Journal for School Administrators, 23*(3), 174–188.

Tobergate, D. R., & Curtis, S. (2002). There is a crisis! And failure is not an option. *Education, 122*(4), 770–776.

Togneri, W. (2003). *Beyond islands of excellence: What districts can do to improve instruction and achievement in all schools—A leadership brief.* Washington, DC: Learning First Alliance.

Tuckman, B. W. (1965). Developmental sequence in small groups. *Psychological Bulletin, 63*(6), 384–399.

U.S. Department of Education (1993). *Office of Research Education Consumer Guide. The Comer School Development Program,* No. 6 (September 1993). Retrieved August 1, 2003, from http://www.ed.gov/pubs/OR/ConsumerGuides/comer.html.

U.S. Department of Education (1994). *Goals 2000: A world-class education for every child.* Washington, DC: Author.

U.S. Department of Education (1995). *Building bridges: The mission and principles of professional development.* Retrieved October 13, 2002, from http://www.ed.gov/G2K/bridge.html.

U.S. Department of Education (1998). *Early warning, timely response: A guide to safe schools.* Retrieved October 13, 2002, from http://cecp.air.org/guide/guide.pdf.

U.S. Department of Education (2002). *Improving Teacher Quality State Grants. Title II, Part A, Non-Regulatory Guidance.* Retrieved February 17, 2003, from http://www.ed.gov/offices/OESE/SIP/TitleIIguidance2002.doc.

U.S. Department of Education (n.d.). *Fact Sheet: The No Child Left Behind Act of (2001).* Retrieved February 17, 2003, from http://www.ed.gov/offices/OESE/esea/factsheet.html.

U.S. Department of Education (n.d.). *Introduction: No Child Left Behind.* Retrieved February 17, 2003, at http://www.nclb.org/next/overview/index.html.

U.S. Department of Education (n.d.) *Improving the Academic Achievement of the Disadvantaged.* Retrieved September 21, 2003, from http://www.ed.gov/policy/elsec/leg/esea02/pg1.html.

U.S. Department of Education. (n.d.). *The No Child Left Behind Act of (2001): Executive Summary.* Retrieved February 17, 2003, from http://www.ed.gov/offices/OESE/esea/exec-summ.html.

Van Heusden Hale, S. (2000). *Comprehensive school reform: Research-based strategies to achieve high standards. A guidebook on school-wide improvement.* San Francisco: WestEd Regional Educational Laboratories.

Wax, E. (2002, June 18). A tough time at the head of the classes. *The Washington Post.* p. 18.

Westheimer, J. (1998). *Among school teachers: Community, autonomy and ideology in teachers' work.* New York: Teachers College Press.

Wheatley, M. (n.d.). *Life affirming leaders. From the four directions: People everywhere leading the way.* Retrieved November 9, 2002 from http://www.fromthefourdirections.org/tpl/ourarticles.tpl

Wheelan, S. A., Tilin, F., & Sanford, J. (1996). School group effectiveness and productivity. *Research/Practice.* Retrieved February 10, 2003, from http://www.coled.umn.edu/CAREI/Reports/Rpractice/Spring96/group.htm.

Wise, A., & Liebbrand, J. (1996). Professional-based accreditation a foundation for high quality teaching. *Phi Delta Kappan, 78*(3), 202–206.

Wood, F. H., & Killian, J. (1998). Job-embedded learning makes the difference in school improvement. *Journal of Staff Development, 19*(1), 52–54.

Woolfolk, A. E. (1990). *Educational psychology* (4th ed.). Englewood Cliffs, NJ: Prentice Hall.

Zepeda, S. J. (1999). *Staff development: Building learning communities.* Larchmont, NY: Eye on Education.

Zepeda, S. J. (2003). *The principal as instructional leader: A handbook for supervisors.* Larchmont, NY: Eye on Education.

Zepeda, S. J., Mayers, R. S., & Benson, B. N. (2003). *The call to teacher leadership.* Larchmont, NY: Eye on Education.